THE SOCIAL PSYCHOLOGY OF EDUCATION

INTERNATIONAL LIBRARY OF SOCIOLOGY AND SOCIAL RECONSTRUCTION

Founded by Karl Mannheim

Editor: W J. H Sprott

A catalogue of the books available in the INTERNATIONAL LIBRARY OF SOCIOLOGY AND SOCIAL RECONSTRUCTION, and new books in preparation for the Library, will be found at the end of this volume.

THE SOCIAL PSYCHOLOGY OF EDUCATION

AN INTRODUCTION AND GUIDE TO ITS STUDY

by

C. M. FLEMING, M.A., Ed.B., Ph.D.

UNIVERSITY OF LONDON INSTITUTE OF EDUCATION

LONDON

ROUTLEDGE & KEGAN PAUL LTD

BROADWAY HOUSE: 68–74 CARTER LANE, E.C.4

First published 1944
Reprinted 1944, 1945, 1947, 1949,
1950, 1951, 1954 and 1957
Second edition (revised) 1959

Reprinted 1963 and 1965

To Managers in Business

To Foremen in Factories

To Leaders in Clubs

To Teachers in Schools

To Parents in Homes

To Husbands. To Wives

To Sisters. To Brothers

To All who have Tried to Educate even on one Day

Printed in Great Britain by Butler & Tanner Ltd., Frome and London

CONTENTS

TO THE READER

THE ability to educate is possessed by you. The desire to educate has been experienced by you. In the pages which follow an attempt is made to describe certain of the conditions under which educating is effected and some of the reasons for its incomplete successes. The words "teacher" and "pupil" are employed freely since these conveniently express the relationship between an educator and one whose behaviour he desires to modify. Their use does not imply that the description is relevant only to educative processes as these are carried out in schools. The problems involved are the same whether their solution is attempted in workshops, in factories, in homes, in schools, in camps or in clubs.

The subject is an important one. Upon the manner in which educating is carried out, and upon the interpretation of human nature on which it is based, depend the issues of ultimate war or peace, of neurotic distresses or mental health, of tyranny or co-operative living in homes, in schools and in workshops—as well as in the larger communities of states or continents.

LONDON, 1963.

PART I

TEACHERS AND THE PUPILS THEY TEACH

CHAPTER I

THE CLASS LOOKS AT THE TEACHER: AN ASSESSMENT OF PERSONALITY

"THERE'S the new teacher. We had him this morning."
"What's he like?"
"Not bad."
"I couldn't hear what he said."
"He looked decent."
"He laughed a lot."
"He didn't see the paper dart I was making."
"He talked too much."
"I'm glad we're to have him."
"Anything's better than the last one."
"Oh, no. He's not so good. I'm not going to work for him."
"He can't write on the blackboard."
"He can't mark a register."
"Perhaps he's a student—not a teacher!"

And so the talk went on as the boys and girls walked out of school. The same sort of talk might have been heard later that same evening when older girls and boys went home from the club and students returned from college. A new teacher is an object of supreme interest to any community of young people; but adults do not always notice the extent of the attentive scrutiny they receive, and rarely do they realise the degree to which youngsters are judges of character and engaged upon the diagnosis of personality.

What means do pupils employ to discover whether the new member of the school group is to be accepted, admired and followed, or rejected, despised and persecuted (in so far as persecution may prove worth while)?

The first method they use is observation of externals—physical characteristics, dress, manner and speech. Pupils prefer teachers to be of their own type—to fall within the limits of the normal as they know it. What those limits are will depend upon their past experiences—their home life and social background. There are no absolute standards. A certain accent may prove a handicap in one district and a social asset in another. Certain mannerisms may irritate some pupils and pass unnoticed by others. Certain physical qualities may excite admiration in one group and attract no particular attention in another. There are also differences in the preferences and expectations of individual pupils. Some will, therefore, admire; some will criticise and many will suspend judgment while they investigate further the qualities of the newcomer.

The second method employed is observation of behaviour. " Does he know the ropes ? " " Has he done it before ? " " Is he nervous ? " " Can he speak so that I can hear him ? " " Are his rate and his voice such that I can listen to him without weariness ? " " Does he notice that I am here ? " " Does he see me ? " " Is he interested in me ? " A successful teacher is accepted by the school community because of his essential oneness with them in certain of their attributes and activities; but they ask more of him than that. They wish also a confidence born of competence and previous experience along the lines on which he proposes to lead them. And they are quite aware that these qualities are revealed partly through visible behaviour; and that the pleasantness of class-room relationships will be greatly increased if the leadership offered is both definite and skilful. They wish also some degree of sympathy. They hope that the new teacher has a mind sufficiently " at leisure from itself " to look out upon them and show awareness of them—a personality able to react and to humour, to laugh with them as well as to guide them.

As a means of discovering the presence of this outward-looking sympathy, pupils use a third method of assessment. They begin to experiment. " Does he mean what he says ? " " What will happen if . . . ? "

This is a most fascinating occupation. It is engaged in by children from very early infancy. It is not unknown to adults in workshop or factory.

" Will he notice if I speak ? " (" Or is he concentrating completely on his own ideas and the subject-matter he wishes to expound ? ") " What will he do ? " " Can he, safely, be made angry ? " (Angry adults are entertaining—though slightly dangerous.)

The circumstances are very similar to those of any controlled experimentation. Miniature situations are deliberately devised. Careful observations are made; and if the teacher proves erratic, ill-informed, or self-absorbed, he has small chance of either acceptance or admiration. The initial attentiveness secured by his novelty will decrease steadily as the group discovers new objects of greater interest and finds another leader more worthy of a following.

The methods employed by pupils in their study of the characteristics of a new teacher are not unlike those standardised in recent years by psychologists engaged on the assessment of temperament, personality or character. They may be summarised as follows:

(1) a study of physical characteristics;

(2) an analysis of expressive movements—voice, gesture, eyes, mouth, gait, carriage, handwriting;

(3) examination of personal expression through speech, writings, dress, possessions, etc.;

(4) observation of conduct and of the frequency of laughter, anger, etc.;

(5) rating of traits by comparison with those of other human beings in the same group;

(6) experiments in miniature situations deliberately devised;

(7) tests of actual persistence, endurance, honesty, self-control, etc., in the course of ordinary living;

(8) a study of social background—family, school, community—in so far as this can be observed.

It is not proposed here to discuss each of these in detail. Many excellent books on the topic are readily accessible.[1] Suffice it to say that such methods are informally and continuously employed in the processes of assessment, interaction and mutual adjustment which form part of the educative influences perpetually exerted by human beings upon one another in the social relationships of the home, the school or the community.

REFERENCES

1. E.g. ALLPORT, G. W., *Personality : A Psychological Interpretation.* Holt, 1937.*

ALLPORT, G. W., *The Nature of Personality.* Addison-Wesley, 1950.

BLAKE, R. R., and RAMSEY, G. V., *Perception : An Approach to Personality.* Ronald Press, 1951.

VERNON, P. E., *Personality Tests and Assessments.* Methuen, 1953.

BREWSTER SMITH, M., BRUNER, J. S., and WHITE, R. W., *Opinions and Personality.* John Wiley, 1956.

* Places of publication are omitted to save space. Names of publishers are given to facilitate identification.

CHAPTER II

THE TEACHER BEGINS TO STUDY THE CLASS: A MEASUREMENT OF INTELLIGENCE

THE teacher, like the pupil, is a student of psychology—trying to understand human nature and human behaviour. And, like the pupil, whatever his other preoccupations, he is engaged upon a continuous assessment of the qualities of the members of the school community.

It is, however, probably true to say that he is more concerned in the first place with the estimation of brightness or intelligence than with the diagnosis of personality or the interpretation of conduct. He is interested in the educability of his pupils. " Will I be able to teach them, to train them, to lead them, to change them ? "

" How do their minds work ? "

" A big class."

" All sorts of youngsters."

" I'll never know them all."

" What shining eyes they have ! "

" A sulky face in the far corner."

" That one talks too much."

" I like the look of the little dark one."

" There's a quick one just beside the door."

" But they're not so bright as last year's group."

Estimation of intelligence has taken certain fairly defined forms —most of which are reflected in the first impressions of any teacher on his first meeting with any class.[1]

Indirect assessments come first—the shape of the face (forehead, nose, chin), the outline of the head (the bumps as they used to be studied by the phrenologists), the expression of the face, physical peculiarities of movement, gait or carriage, the nature of the hands, the bodily proportions in general. Such things, to a greater or less degree, are regularly noted by most people as a means towards the prediction of probable performance; and it is not surprising that in the history of intelligence testing observations of this type represented the first steps in objective estimation. In the latter part of the nineteenth century such descriptions of physical characteristics were supplemented by investigations into the powers of the body as shown in sensory discrimination and accurate movement. And at a still later date these investigations were followed by researches based on the expectation that brighter pupils would show greater accuracy and speed in the exercise of various powers of the mind. Mental qualities were more and more judged by mental symptoms.

The teacher face to face with a new class does not, of course, pause to realise that he is following the course taken by several generations of research workers; but he does judge his pupils first by their looks and their movements and only later—as he comes to know them better—by an assessment of their performance.

"How much of this can you remember?"

"What did you see when I said that word?"

"Say these words after me."

"Say these numbers after me."

"Look at this drawing. I am going to ask you to reproduce it for me from memory."

"How quickly can you do this exercise?"

"Which of these things has no connection with the others?"

"What is the meaning of this word?"

"Is there anything silly in this statement?"

"Which is the biggest of these numbers?"

"Arrange these in order of weight."

"This is older than that and that is twice as old as these. Which is the oldest?"

Tests of memory, of visual imagery, and of attention were followed by tests devised to measure reasoning ability and the use of the mind in classification, definition, detection of absurdities, comparison, arrangements of ideas in sequence, deduction and the like.[2]

Much material of this kind is inevitably included in the ordinary experiences of classroom or club—almost irrespective of the actual subject-matter under review—and little by little the outlines of the picture are filled in. The teacher comes to believe that he knows his class. "Nothing they do will surprise me. I now know them through and through."

There are, however, two disturbing factors. A teacher may make mistakes. He may entertain a prejudice against red hair, a Roman nose, slow responses, a garrulous tongue; and, influenced by such things, he may condemn a pupil to undeserved neglect. A teacher also may be—and usually is—very closely confined to one classroom or one club. He does make comparisons. "This class is on the whole better-looking than the group I had last year." "These club members are less friendly than those." His comparisons, however, are within a very narrow framework. They are subjective—dependent upon his own passing opinion. They lack objectivity and impartiality.

The same sort of difficulty is encountered in the assessment of achievement. A teacher, for example, having worked with a class for a term, sets an examination and (full of hope) proceeds to the marking of the results. The first papers he reads are very poor. One pupil after another is incomprehensibly stupid and ill-informed. It is most depressing. Then a change occurs. The later responses are much more sensible. The second half of the class gains marks distinctly above those accorded to the first half.

It is possible, of course, that the papers of the weaker pupils happened to be collected at the top of the pile. Or it may have been that Mr. Jones, who did the marking, changed his standard as he worked through the bundle. Evidence on these possibilities can very readily be secured by re-marking each paper—beginning on the second occasion with those which were dealt with at the end of the first assessment. Estimation of the average of the two marks so obtained will probably go far to eliminate internal inconsistency.

It may have been, however, that the class was a very poor class (or that Mr. Jones was a very severe marker). Evidence on this can be got only by comparison with other classes and with the scores given by other examiners.

Such comparison of standards of achievement and of assessment can now be made with much more certainty than was possible a few decades ago. It is not necessary here to describe the researches that have contributed to this development.[3] Suffice it to say that three observations have made it possible:

(1) Tests can be tested by trying them on representative samples in comparable groups.
(2) Test results of representative samples when graphed fall roughly into a shape which has been described as the curve of normal frequency.
(3) The validity of a measure can be estimated by comparison of its results with those of some other accepted test; and the reliability of a test can be judged by its internal consistency (through comparison of alternate answers or estimation of the degree of its correspondence with itself on repetition).

Before testing children with a test it seems only reasonable to test the test on children. Before saying that a normal ten-year-old "should" be able to answer a certain question, it seems a simple matter to think of trying the question on a representative group of similar pupils of comparable age, country and circumstances. If about three-quarters of the ten-year-old pupils can answer it, it seems fair to say that it is a question suitable for pupils of "mental age" ten. Such a procedure had been suggested in the latter part of the nineteenth century, but it was not until the first years of the twentieth century that Binet popularised the proposal. Since then a technique has been devised which has made possible the construction of " scales " for skills such as composition, writing and drawing and of tests for abilities such as reading, arithmetic, spelling, manual dexterity or general intellectual competence.

This technique includes the application of the second and third observation mentioned above. A very simple experiment will demonstrate the normal scatter of representative test results. If a randomly selected group of pupils be asked to make dots in rows on a piece of paper for thirty seconds . . . . . . it will be found that very few tap very slowly, very few attain the maximum rate and the majority make a record which falls somewhere in the middle.

The same sort of distribution is found when objective measurement is made of almost any human attribute—mental, physical, social or emotional—in an unselected sample of the population. It may be expected to appear if the construction and the marking of a new test have made it largely independent of the personal prejudice, the inconsistency or the limited experience of the teacher or the examiner.

By graphing results a teacher can discover to what extent the scores of his group seem to conform to the distribution of normal frequency. By comparing his distribution with that obtained from the use of a test already standardised he can obtain some idea of the suitability of his examination and the impartiality of the assessment he has made. The development of statistical formulæ by which the degree of correspondence or relationship between two such measures can be expressed in mathematical symbols (instead of in mere verbal descriptions) has done much to render possible a science of human measurement. Through use of the findings of this science [4] a teacher can escape from the limitations consequent on his own confinement in one classroom as well as from the uncertainties of his own judgment with its known liability to personal bias.

REFERENCES

1. For a lucid description of these see—
   FREEMAN, F. S., *Theory and Practice of Psychological Testing.* Henry Holt, 1950.
   ANASTASI, A., *Psychological Testing.* Macmillan, 1954.
   VERNON, P. E., *Intelligence and Attainment Tests.* Univ. of London Press, 1960.
2. For an account of nineteenth-century experiments see—
   WHIPPLE, G. M., *Manual of Mental and Physical Tests.* Warwick and York. 1910 ;

and for specimens and discussion of twentieth-century tests see—

VERNON, P.E., *loc. cit.*, and

VERNON, P. E., *The Measurement of Abilities.* Univ. of London Press, 1940 and 1956.

BUROS, O. K., *Mental Measurements Yearbook.* Rutgers Univ. Press, 1938 and 1941, 1949, 1953.

3. Excellent accounts may be found in—

CRONBACH, L. J., *Essentials in Psychological Testing.* Harper Brothers, 1949.

LINDQUIST, E. F. (ed.), *Educational Measurement.* American Council on Education, 1951.

THORNDIKE, R. L., and HAGEN, E., *Measurement and Evaluation in Psychology and Education.* John Wiley, 1955.

4. For discussion of statistical methods see VERNON, P. E., *loc. cit.*

DAWSON, S., *An Introduction to the Computation of Statistics.* Univ. of London Press, 1933.

CHAMBERS, E. G., *Statistical Calculations for Beginners.* Cambridge Univ. Press, 1940.

GUILFORD, J. P., *Fundamental Statistics in Psychology and Education.* McGraw-Hill, 1942 and 1950.

JOHNSON, P. O., and JACKSON, R. B., *Introduction to Statistical Methods.* Prentice-Hall, 1953.

CHAPTER III

A DIGRESSION ON INSTINCTS AND RELATED TOPICS

A TEACHER'S first question when he faces a new class may have been, " How do their minds work ? " His second (and it comes with great speed) is, " What sort of human beings are they ? " A similar progression may be traced (by those who are interested in such sequences) in the history and content of psychology.

" Psychology " began by being a study of mind. Through many centuries it was an off-shoot from philosophy and metaphysics. Its emphasis was on the nature of mind and the processes involved in thinking. Its methods were those of theorising and introspection. Only towards the end of the nineteenth century did it turn wholeheartedly towards observation of individuals, recording of behaviour, and experimentation ; and it is no accident that it is only since the beginning of the twentieth century that it has received the status of an independent study in most of the Universities of the world.

" What sort of human beings are they ? " " What are human beings like ? " To answer these questions the teacher (like psychologists in general before him) often looks first at the individuals who make up his class. What are their attributes or characteristics ? They can feel, perceive, understand, imagine, judge, reason, remember, act. They have sensations, perceptions, thoughts, imagination, judgment, reasoning, memory, will-power. From the earliest recorded discussions up to those of the end of the nineteenth century the main interest of educators seems to have centred upon such " faculties " and their employment in the educative process.[1]

Teaching was assumed to be concerned with training in the use of mental faculties ; and books on psychology dealt with subjects such as sensation, perception, cognition, imagination, memory, reasoning, attention, will. Mention was also made of emotions and impulses, but relatively little emphasis was laid upon these, and their importance for the educator was believed to be small. Information upon all these topics was amassed by introspection, and generalisations were supported by observation of humanity from the safe shelter of a library or a study.

Towards the end of the nineteenth century, however, for a variety of reasons, writers upon education became more interested in what is now called " clinical " study. Psychologists founded "laboratories", and began to apply methods of exact observation and controlled experiment to the study of psychology and (at a much later date) to education. The first psychological clinics were opened. Teachers brought pupils—at first as "subjects" for experimentation and later as "patients" who might be helped in the light of the findings of the new "child study". Some young psychologists began to concern themselves with experiments on animals. Others took training as physiologists and others turned back to psychology after qualifying as alienists or specialists in criminology.[2] From all these other sciences something was learnt, and almost insensibly the connotation of the word "psychology" changed and its field widened to that of the study of human nature as a whole.

One consequence of this change in viewpoint was an increased interest in inherited characteristics and innate endowment. Behaviour which is commonly called instinctive is readily observable amongst animals. It was assumed that a comparable innate, universal or instinctive pattern of behaviour characterised human beings; and, in the early years of the twentieth century, enthusiastic study was therefore given to instincts such as—

the parental or protective instincts,
the instinct of appeal,
the food-seeking instinct,
the mating instinct,
the gregarious instinct,
the instinct of combat,
the acquisitive instinct.
the instinct of curiosity,
the constructive instinct,
the instinct of repulsion,
the instinct of escape,
the instinct of self-assertion,
the instinct of submission.

The most popular exponent of the new point of view among British and American psychologists was probably McDougall;[3] but its influence may be traced in the writings of William James, Burt, Drever, and many others; and its effect may be noticed in discussions on education in books by such British workers as Nunn, Ross, Hughes, Hadfield.[4]

The meaning given to the word "instinct" in most of these discussions is clearly defined by Burt in the opening article of an early symposium published in the *British Journal of Educational Psychology*[5]—

a complex inherited tendency, common to all members of a species, impelling each individual (1) to perceive and pay attention to certain objects or situations, (2) to become pleasurably or unpleasurably excited about those objects whenever they are perceived, and (3) thereupon to act in a way likely in the long run to preserve the individual, or at any rate the species, so acting.

The importance of the concept was that it permitted some explanation to be given of human activity, and of the sudden outbursts of energy and emotional excitement which are observable characteristics of human behaviour. The things or events that provoke such outbursts were held to derive their power from the fact that they appealed to primitive instincts; and these instincts (inherited from animal ancestors) were believed to form the foundation of individual character as well as the commonest sources of crime. The task of the teacher was to make allowances for them, utilise them and adapt all educative endeavours to them.

This emphasis on instinctive forces and impulses—unpremeditated, unreasoning and imperfectly understood—provided a most valuable corrective to the excessively intellectual approach of earlier writers and led to increased awareness of the need for the study of emotions as well as of ideas—of feelings and unconscious motives in addition to deliberate intentions and ideals. Teachers and parents became more alive to the complexity of their responsibilities; and it became more usual to admit the occurrence of behaviour which appeared to be irrational and of whose origins the individual was unaware. This was a great advance upon mere philosophic meditation upon mental faculties. It may be noted, however, that it was in essence an emphasis on "original nature" and, while it provided a practicable scheme of classification and inference, it was based upon the study of individuals as things-in-themselves, observable as separate entities. It encouraged a labelling of individuals as timid, aggressive, submissive, repressed, conscious of inferiority, self-centred or introverted, outward-looking or extraverted, and it led to an emphasis on the inherited character, the consistency and the fixity of such behaviour patterns. It was assumed, for example, that from the behaviour of a child's brothers, sisters or parents it was possible to infer what would probably be the child's own behaviour even when the training and the social influences to which he had been submitted had been altered or improved, that because a child started and turned pale at a sudden noise he would therefore probably be afraid of large animals, of strange human beings, of novel situations and of all the other stimuli for fear, and that his behaviour at later stages would in such respects closely resemble his behaviour in early infancy. Troublesome behaviour was accounted for as arising mainly from the excessive intensity with which one or more of these emotional impulses had been inherited by a particular individual; while temperamental apathy was believed to result from an innate condition in which the fundamental instincts and emotions were too weak and inert.[6]

Such consistency, fixity and independence of environment do not, however, on closer inspection, characterise the behaviour of children in most families and most schools. Human beings do not always remain in the categories in which they are placed; and clinical psychologists have had to admit that the same individual may in one set of relationships appear as aggressive and in another as submissive—in one situation he may be an introvert and in another an extravert. A pupil may be conscious of inferiority in a gymnasium and of superiority in a class-room. He may be timid in a situation involving swimming and bold on the football field. He may appear shy and repressed in one set of circumstances and excitable and assertive in another. His behaviour patterns may also change as the years pass. He may become better adjusted, more balanced, more resolute; and in all these respects an orphan may appear to resemble very slightly the parents he has never known.

In consequence it has had to be acknowledged [7] that human instincts are " pliant and uncertain tendencies, seeds that may never spring up " and that neither delinquency nor neurosis is due exclusively to inborn constitution nor yet to shocks and maladjustments in the remote past, but may spring largely out of contemporaneous conditions and conflicts.

These observations of clinical psychologists have been confirmed by anthropological and sociological studies of the differing behaviour-patterns which are observable in different societies and in different ages.[8] The terms used by writers in discussion of instincts are useful enough as descriptive of the various potentialities of human beings. They are misleading and inadequate when applied, as they often are, as explanatory of the wide variety of responses to comparable situations in different centuries or in different districts. Much behaviour which used to be called instinctive is therefore now considered to be more fairly described as " learned "—built up or " conditioned " by the experiences to which an individual has been subjected. Many of the similarities which are observable seem to be accompanied by recognisable similarities in environment; while differences appear to be concomitant with different traditions and different material surroundings.

It may be of interest to note that, with the support of such psychological and sociological evidence, a comparable criticism has, for similar reasons, in recent years been directed against Freudian interpretations of the results of psycho-analysis. It is unnecessary here (and would be somewhat irrelevant) to describe in detail the history and the development of Freud's technique or the skill with which he drew popular attention to the significance of the unconscious in human thought and action. Suffice it to say that his has been one of the most influential of the instinctivistic schools of psychology—particularly in countries where other theories of instinctive motivation were strongly emphasised.[9] His interpretation took a highly specialised form; but in essence his method was that of a doctor treating a patient as an individual in a consulting-room.

He admitted the importance of environmental handling in the first few years of life, but over-emphasised the biological origins of present behaviour; and he laid too slight a stress on present attitudes, interests and wishes in their relation to the social group of which an individual forms a part. Man to him was fundamentally anti-social, absorbed in the search for gratification of biological drives; and the task of the educator was to suppress as far as necessary certain basic impulses which were postulated as fixed and as virtually the same in every member of the species.

With other psychologists of the opening years of the twentieth century, Freud played an important part in reaffirming the reality of emotional conflict, and re-emphasising the difficulties involved in modifying human behaviour; but his individualised methods are now being supplemented by group methods utilising the therapeutic value of impersonal discussion of common problems [10] or superseded by studies which rely upon observation and treatment of the child in the nursery, the person in his family, or the worker in and through his occupation.[11]

Study of human beings as organisms with instinctive tendencies is important as a reminder of the probable limits of educability. Observation of the behaviour of these organisms in varying situations is even more relevant to the understanding of human nature as it functions amid the realities of home life or school life. The teacher, the parent and the psychologist, in so far as they observe life as a whole, have to pass from a study of individuals seen one by one at any given time to an awareness of individual behaviour as it appears in the shifting groups, and changing social relationships which characterise a school, a home, or a community.*

* The use of the word "instinct" in descriptions of behaviour—whether of human beings or of animals—has too often been followed by a cessation of observation and a stifling of the spirit of enquiry. It seems desirable to substitute for this word a descriptive term whose content carries less emphasis on individual past behaviour and hypothetical "original nature" and is less liable to lead to the assumption that little can be done in the way of modification of present outstanding characteristics.

REFERENCES

1. For a useful account of the faculty theory as it was applied to education see BURT, C., *Historical Note on Faculty Psychology.* Report of the Consultative Committee on Secondary Education, Appendix IV. H.M.S.O., 1938.
Cf. BODE, B. H., *Conflicting Psychologies of Learning.* Harrap, 1929.
For examples of tests constructed under its influence see WHIPPLE, *loc. cit.*
2. For interesting examples of these excursions cf. MURCHISON, C. (ed.), *A History of Psychology in Autobiography.* Clark University Press, 1931.
3. MCDOUGALL, W., *An Introduction to Social Psychology.* Methuen, 1908.
DREVER, J., *Instinct in Man.* Cambridge Univ. Press, 1917.
MCDOUGALL, W., *An Outline of Psychology.* Methuen, 1923.
BURT, C., *The Young Delinquent.* Univ. of London Press, 1925.
4. NUNN, T. P., *Education : Its Data and First Principles.* Edward Arnold, 1920.
HADFIELD, J. A., *Psychology and Morals.* Methuen, 1923.
ROSS, J. S., *Groundwork of Educational Psychology.* Harrap, 1931.
HUGHES, A. G., and HUGHES, E. H., *Learning and Teaching.* Longmans Green, 1937 ; and
BURT, C., *The Backward Child.* Univ. of London Press, 1937.
5. BURT, C., *The Case for Human Instincts,* " British Journal of Educational Psychology ", XI, 1941, pp. 155–72.
VERNON, P. E., *Some Objections to the Theory of Human Instincts,* ibid., XII, 1942, pp. 1–9.
THORNDIKE, E. L., *Human Instincts and Doctrines about Them,* ibid., XII, 1942, pp. 85–7.
DREVER, J., *Instinct as Impulse,* ibid., XII, 1942, pp. 88–96.
PEAR, T. H., *Not Dead, but Obsolescent ?* ibid., XII, 1942, pp. 139–47.
MYERS, C. S., *Retrospect and Prospect,* ibid., XII, 1942, pp. 148–55.
BURT, C., *Conclusion,* ibid., XIII, 1943, pp. 1–15.
See also:
ALLEE, W. C., NISSEN, H. W., and NIMKOFF, M. F., *A Re-examination of the Concept of Instinct,* " Psychol. Bull.", 60, 5, pp. 287–97, 1953.
BEACH, F. A., *The Descent of Instinct,* " Psychol. Rev.", 62, 6, pp. 401–10, 1955.
6. cf. BURT, C., *loc. cit.*, 1937, pp. 541, 555, and *loc. cit.*, 1941, p. 165.
7. *v.* BURT, C., *loc. cit.*, 1925, p. 526, and compare
BURT, C., *The Subnormal Mind.* Oxford Univ. Press, 1937, p. 185.
8. *v.* MEAD, M., *Coming of Age in Samoa* and *Growing Up in New Guinea.* Penguin Reprints, 1943 ; and
MEAD, M., *The Primitive Child,* in MURCHISON, C. (ed.), *A Handbook of Child Psychology.* Clark Univ. Press, 1933.
cf. SUTTIE, I. D., *The Origins of Love and Hate.* Kegan Paul, 1935.
FROMM, E., *The Fear of Freedom.* Kegan Paul, 1942.
KARDINER, A., *et al., The Psychological Frontiers of Society.* Columbia Univ. Press, 1945.
9. The most accessible of Freud's books is one of the earliest : *The Psycho-Pathology of Everyday Life* (1901)—translated into English in 1914 and reprinted in 1938 as a Penguin Special. Useful accounts of his views are given in :
FREUD, S., *Introductory Lectures on Psycho-Analysis.* Allen & Unwin, 1922.

FREUD, S., *New Introductory Lectures on Psycho-Analysis.* Hogarth Press, 1933.
FREUD, S., *An Autobiographical Study.* Hogarth Press, 1935.
HENDRICK, I., *Facts and Theories of Psycho-Analysis.* Kegan Paul, 1934.
HOLLITSCHER, W., *Sigmund Freud : An Introduction.* Kegan Paul, 1947.
Books on educational psychology and the upbringing of children from the psycho-analytic point of view include :
ISAACS, S., *The Children We Teach.* Univ. of London Press, 1932.
RICKMAN, J. R., *On the Bringing up of Children.* Kegan Paul, 1936.
MILLER, E., *et al., The Growing Child and its Problems.* Kegan Paul, 1937.
GORDON, R. G., *A Survey of Child Psychiatry.* Oxford Univ. Press, 1939.
BOWLEY, A. H., *The Natural Development of the Child.* E. S. Livingstone, 1942.
FRIEDLANDER, K., *The Psycho-analytic Approach to Juvenile Delinquency.* Kegan Paul, 1947.
Their study can be supplemented by surveys such as those in :
MURPHY, G., *An Historical Introduction to Modern Psychology.* Kegan Paul, 1929.
MORGAN, J. J. B., *The Psychology of Abnormal People.* Longmans Green, 1940,
and by the discussions of other psycho-therapists exemplified by books such as :
ADLER, A., *Understanding Human Nature.* Allen & Unwin, 1930.
ADLER, A., *Guiding Human Misfits.* Macmillan, 1938.
REES, J. R., *The Health of the Mind.* Faber & Faber, 1929.
SUTTIE, I. D., *The Origins of Love and Hate.* Kegan Paul, 1935.
BROWN, W., *Psychological Methods of Healing.* Univ. of London Press, 1938.
HORNEY, K., *New Ways in Psycho-Analysis.* Kegan Paul, 1939.
ROGERS, C. R., *Counseling and Psychotherapy.* Houghton Mifflin, 1942.
ROGERS, C. R., *Client-Centered Therapy.* Houghton Mifflin, 1951.
10. For an accessible discussion and list of references—
v. BIERER, J., *Group Psychotherapy,* " British Medical Journal ", Feb. 14th, 1942.
MORENO, J. L., *Who Shall Survive?* Nervous and Mental Disease Publishing Co., 1934 and Beacon House, 1953.
MORENO, J. L. (ed.), *Group Psychotherapy : A Symposium.* Beacon House Inc., 1945.
11. cf. HORNEY, K., *New Ways in Psycho-Analysis.* Kegan Paul, 1939; and ROGERS, C. R., *Clinical Treatment of the Problem Child.* Houghton Mifflin, 1939.*
BIERER, J. (ed.), *Therapeutic Social Clubs.* H. K. Lewis [n.d.].
BIERER, J., *The Day Hospital.* H. K. Lewis, 1951.

* The almost imperceptible shift of interest among psychologists from a preoccupation with the classification of impulses and instincts to a greater awareness of the complexity and fluidity of social relationships may be seen through a comparison of reports published about 1925 with records of similar origin whose published date is a dozen years later. (In similar fashion an earlier zeal for the assessment of the relative influence of inheritance and environment has been succeeded by a study of the emotional and social factors accompanying observable human development.)

CHAPTER IV

NEEDS AND THEIR SATISFACTIONS

A TEACHER'S first question often is, "How do their minds work?" His second may be, "What sort of pupil is this one?" His third and ultimate question has to be, "What sort of human beings are these pupils as I really meet them in a group—as individuals in relation to other individuals?"[1]

The study of intellect, of mental faculties and of instincts provided some answer to the first and to the second question. An enquiry into needs and their satisfaction is a sequel to the attempt to understand human beings as members of groups.

What are the chief human needs? On the physical plane they are probably food, warmth and shelter; and the importance of suitable satisfaction of these requirements is becoming more apparent to educators as a result of medical research in the State schools. It is not, however, directly the concern of the individual teacher in his own class-room. On the physiological plane the comparable requirements are the satisfaction of physiological appetites such as hunger, thirst, rest and change. Training of these is coming increasingly within the sphere of the teacher's responsibility.

On the psychological plane various answers have been given and it is significant that their clearest expression has come from clinicians concerned with the treatment of delinquent youths or problem children.[2] These young people are in difficulties. What differences can be discovered between their experiences and their characteristics and relationships and those of the other youngsters who are called normal or well-behaved? One of the earliest accessible formulations was given in 1920 by W. I. Thomas in a report entitled "The Unadjusted Girl". Delinquency was described by him not as a consequence of perverted personal characteristics—physical or psychological—but as an absence of adjustment by the individual to the demands of society and as a sequel to the failure of society to satisfy the basic needs or "wishes" of the individual.

Those wishes were formulated as:

(1) the desire for new experience,
(2) the desire for security,
(3) the desire for response,
(4) the desire for recognition.

The conception is a fruitful one. What are the chief needs of a human being? The first is probably that of security.

This requires not mere freedom from want but acceptance by the group whose affection, approval and admiration are necessary to wholesome growth. Evidence on the consequences of the absence or the loss of such security is accumulating in records from law courts, from studies of evacuated youngsters in war-time, and from observations of the behaviour of pupils who have suffered long series of scholastic defeats in schools still shadowed by over-emphasis on uniformity among pupils of unequal endowment.

Thwarting of the need to give and to receive affection in the first few months of life has been found to be associated with delinquent behaviour at later stages; and awareness of lack of interest and affection on the part of foster-parents or teachers has been noticed to transform apparently normal children into unhappy and over-anxious neurotics.[3] (The neurotic distresses of conscripts are now being accounted for in similar fashion; and emphasis in the discussion of what used to be called "shell-shock" is shifting from Freudian interpretations of conflicting instincts to a consideration of suitable methods of re-education and reconditioning designed to lessen "separation-anxiety" and to render recruits aware of their position in the larger "family circle" of the regiment, the army or the nation.)

A sense of security seems to be strengthened also by experiences of orderly living. It is important that personal relationships should be such that there is a deep awareness of acceptance and affection along with opportunities for the manifestation of reciprocal tenderness. It is necessary, in addition, that life be lived in a reasonably stable environment where physical needs are met with sufficient regularity and where budding confidence is not stifled by capricious cruelties, inconsistencies and tyrannies. The normal routine of most homes satisfies these requirements and the same need for stability is met by the traditional orderliness of most school programmes.

After security comes the need for adventure—for fresh things to do, fresh interests, fresh knowledge. This need for opportunities of growth is met in varying ways at different stages in development. To the little child the simplest progressions in learning provide adequate satisfaction—from crawling to standing, from standing to walking, from walking to running and climbing and balancing. To the child at school (if the teacher is wise) the same sort of thrill can be provided by the gradual conquest of new skills of varied kinds; and from each successive achievement an awareness of the recognition and admiration of the group comes to fortify the courage resulting from acceptance in an orderly universe combined with satisfactory excursions into the unknown. At a later stage these same needs are met by vocations, occupations, hobbies, games, by leisure pursuits of various kinds—and also by the adventures among ideas which in their most abstract form are called philosophy or metaphysics.

A third human need is the one which may be described as the need for personal independence through the agency of something over which responsibility can be exercised. At an early stage this shows itself in the need for possessions. The effect of lack of personal belongings is frequently observable among delinquent children convicted of theft. An understanding of what is called " respect for property " can be acquired only by those who have had some possessions of their own over which they have exercised responsibility and which have in turn been respected by others. The actual nature of the possessions is of little moment. They may range in type from collections of bus tickets, of stamps, pebbles, or nails to toys, books, clothes and, later, household equipment or land. The human need behind the impulse to acquire such things is the same. They are valued partly as a means of strengthening security and partly as a device for increasing self-respect and ensuring social approval. Their importance is not measurable in terms of the instinctive urges of an individual. It is essentially a social matter—relative to the position desired by an individual in a group and determined by his need for recognition as an independent entity in the group.

Security, adventure, responsibility—all these are human needs ; and in so far as a teacher can meet these needs he may be said to be co-operating with his pupils and not working against them. To the degree to which he does this, success is likely to crown his labours.

Observation of the means by which such fundamental needs meet satisfaction or frustration now forms a large part of the subject-matter of educational psychology ; and in succeeding chapters constant reference will be made to social relationships and the interplay of individuals and groups in a variety of situations involving learning and teaching. Their fuller treatment here in those connections seems therefore unnecessary. It may be noted, however, that the same issues are involved in other social problems which are not so frequently thought of as similar in character.

At the pre-school level, for example, the question is sometimes debated as to whether infants should be reared in institutions or in homes. A few years ago, developments in the knowledge of the means by which diseases are transmitted led to an emphasis on the importance of isolation, of segregation, and of the minimum of handling by adults who were possibly infected with a variety of germs. In spite of precautions taken in the light of such knowledge, it had, however, to be admitted that, on the whole, infants pined physically when attended by masked nurses in completely hygienic cubicles, and bloomed when restored to the dangers of their mothers' arms. Similar emotional disadvantages were observed to result from impersonal handling in residential nurseries. The institution infant showed less development in social responsiveness, less obvious happiness, less confidence, and less stability. At later stages he suffered from anxieties consequent upon premature exposure to the unthinking aggressiveness of his peers [4]—in the absence of the sense of protection which follows from a knowledge of the love of even one important adult. Experimentation showed that some improvement could be effected if individual attention was given by one nurse over a long period, and also that better social maturing and greater mental health followed the removal of orphans to suitable foster-homes. The physical conditions of the residential schools or institutions had probably been better than those of such foster homes. The children in them had had more chances of exercise in the open air. Food had often been more carefully selected and equipment more suitable. These material and physical advantages were, however, more than counterbalanced by the absence of family life and the loss of fundamental emotional satisfactions.

Similar handicaps may be suffered by children whose home-life is superficially normal. Edna was the child of rich parents. She was brought every morning to a private Nursery School by an imposing chauffeur in an impressive car. She was extremely "well-behaved". She would sit quietly in a corner for hours on end with neither movement nor speech—so long as no notice was taken of her. If spoken to, she would hang her head. If touched unexpectedly, she would scream. If asked to do anything, she would cry. No co-operation or social contacts could be secured. Enquiry showed that she had been brought up by a succession of nurses who had accustomed her to passivity in a cot and in a play-pen. Toys had been provided; but no real opportunities for play had been given. No one had ever shown her affection. The first task of the nursery school was to awaken an awareness of tenderness. Its second was to revive a desire for adventures.

Bob was a somewhat grubby newcomer at an Infant School. He lived in a poor neighbourhood; but he appeared to be sufficiently well-nourished and hardy. In the playground he ran about with the others; but in the class-room he refused to speak. Examination showed no physical or mental defect; but a visit to the home revealed that no one had troubled to talk to him. He had been an unwanted baby. His mother could not get rid of him. She had fed him and dressed him and left him to his own devices. He had learnt the meaning of adult speech; but had had no encouragement towards utterance, and his own vocabulary was limited to the phrases needed in street games and in very simple requests for food. He also was unresponsive, timid, sulky and anti-social. The abnormalities of both children were related not so much to their material environment, their intelligence or their instinctive tendencies as to their defective social relationships and the personal frustrations they had encountered. Both had suffered from loneliness in infancy and a lack of opportunities to give and to receive affection. Both were insecure and unco-operative.

Comparable observations have been made in studies of civilian morale both in unemployment and in industry.[5] Higher morale during unemployment was found, for example, to have been maintained by those who had known emotional security in childhood, had had fuller educational opportunities, a consequent greater range of interests, and more experience of recognition and success. Greater resistance to the effects of the economic depression was also shown by those who had previously shouldered responsibilities—whether in the form of holding office in clubs or in the establishment of a home or the support of a family. Intelligence, good health and adequate nutrition were important contributory conditions; but differences in these seemed on the whole less significant than differences in the satisfactions of the basic human needs for acceptance, affection, a variety of experiences and the social recognition consequent upon possession of a position of some responsibility.

Studies of morale in industry show similar findings. The spirit and the attitude of workers seem determined less by the actual payment received or the physical conditions under which work is done than by the social relationships implicit in the treatment given by foremen or supervisors. Autocratic bosses, officials who criticise and scold, and workshops in which there are few opportunities for responsibility or experiment produce workers who are "apathetic", "lazy", "irresponsible" and "clumsy". Labour-turnover in such places is excessive; and personal initiative and interest are low. Changes in attitudes and social relationships can, however (even among adult workers), produce remarkable changes in morale. Re-education in industry is by no means impossible.

Comparable education in public opinion is also quite possible. It is constantly being attempted through the use of those visual and verbal means which are described as "advertisements". Propagation of opinions is achieved not through a training in perceiving, in memorising, in attention, in visual imagery or in imagination (as psychologists used to assume); but through the offering of some satisfaction of the primary human needs—of the wish for social acceptance, for membership of an admired group, for fresh adventures, new ideas, a consciousness of personal responsibility and (to a lesser extent) a defence of personal possessions. (The last-mentioned, it may be noticed, is the least effective and the most readily sacrificed for the sake of other values and other wishes.) "Your country needs you." "A wife to be proud of." "Join us and see the world." "You can help."

Similar explanations can be offered of the greater degree of happiness and mental health achieved by those who are actively aware of religious experience, and their greater resistance to disappointments, persecutions, loss of work, reduction of income and the like. Morale is known to be reduced by an interruption in religious observances, and has been observed to be higher in those groups in which there is active membership of religious organisations.[5]

REFERENCES

1. It may be remarked here that illustrative references throughout are to actual cases whose identity is suitably concealed.
2. THOMAS, W. I., *The Unadjusted Girl.* Little Brown, 1920.
   SUTTIE, I. D., *The Origins of Love and Hate.* Kegan Paul, 1935.
   HAMLEY, H. R., *et al., The Education of Backward Children.* Evans, 1936.
   ROGERS, C. R., *The Clinical Treatment of the Problem Child.* Houghton Mifflin, 1939.
   MOODIE, W., *The Doctor and the Difficult Child.* Commonwealth Fund, 1940.
3. cf. PADLEY, R., and COLE, N. (ed.). *Evacuation Survey.* Routledge, 1940.
   BURT, C., *The Incidence of Neurotic Symptoms among Evacuated School Children,* "British Journal of Educational Psychology", X, 1, 1940, pp. 10–15.
   VERNON, M. D., *A Study of Some Effects of Evacuation on Adolescent Girls,* ibid., X, 2, 1940, pp. 114–34.
   ISAACS, S. (ed.), *The Cambridge Evacuation Survey.* Methuen, 1941.
   VERNON, P. E., *The Psychological Effects of Air-Raids,* "Journal of Abnormal and Social Psychology", XXXVI, 1941, pp. 457–76.
   WOLF, K. M., *Evacuation of Children in Wartime.* A Survey. "Psycho-anal. Study of Child", I, pp. 389–404, 1945.
   FLEMING, C. M., *Teaching : A Psychological Analysis.* Methuen and John Wiley, 1958.
4. cf. FREUD, A., and BURLINGHAM, D., *Early Relations between Residential Infants,* "New Era", July 24, 1943, pp. 119–25.
5. cf. WATSON, GOODWIN, *Morale during Unemployment* in *Civilian Morale.* Houghton Mifflin, 1942.

CHAPTER V

THE CHANGING OF BEHAVIOUR: INDIVIDUALS CAN MODIFY GROUPS

FROM one point of view the educative process may be said to include all the means by which the behaviour of human beings is modified through their contact with other human beings—either directly or indirectly. (The learning process is much wider than this and includes changes attributable to maturing and to reactions to alterations in the physical environment.) Education does not, of course, take place only in schools. It does not result only from deliberate instruction or teaching. It is observable wherever modifications occur—whether they are modifications resulting from influences exerted by individuals on other individuals (or on groups) or changes consequent on the social pressure employed by groups in their handling of individuals. In both instances, the alterations produced may be modifications in knowledge (through the types of behaviour commonly described as memorising, analysing or reproducing). They may be changes in skill (in bodily habits, or activities). They may be modifications in values, attitudes and interests.

It may be useful to consider first the changes initiated by individuals. These may affect other individuals (or groups) through face-to-face contacts such as are experienced in the family circle, in schools and in community-agencies like clubs or churches. They may, on the other hand, reach their objective indirectly through books, through broadcasting, or through the visual education given by films or advertisements. Whatever the media employed, it is to be noted that their effect depends not merely on the skill with which their appeal is devised, or the absolute attractiveness of their form or content. It depends also on the nature of the response of the individual (or the group) to whom their appeal is addressed. To some instructions or educative influences, an individual is receptive or responsive. To others he is indifferent, and to others he may react by rejection or refusal. The exact nature of the response depends not merely upon his original nature and endowment (though these have their importance). It is not a mere sequel to his past experiences in general. It varies with his present intentions and wishes, and also with his social relationships to the individual who is responsible for the attempt to " educate ".

The issues involved can be readily observed in the responses of a mixed company to an advertisement, an announcement on a notice board, a warning from a pulpit, or an instruction from a school platform. Identical orders may be given by different teachers to the same group. In one case they may provoke antagonism. In another they may appear entirely without effect. Coming from a third teacher they may arouse enthusiastic acceptance.

To what are these differences due? A partial answer may be found in discussions of what psychologists have called "suggestion".

The learning processes involved in genuine suggestion are more complex than the mere consequences of listening to a statement or receiving an instruction.[1] They include a heightened attentiveness, with an accompanying emotion and a subconscious continuation of a belief which was begun with greater or lesser awareness. They depend also upon attitudes, interests and values; and their effect is therefore closely related to the prestige or acceptance accorded to the source to which they are accredited.

A simple example may make this clear. A pupil who has just begun attendance at school is peculiarly open to the working of suggestion. Ted Jackson was in this position. He had arrived at school full of anticipations of pleasure and expectations of success. All went well for some weeks. He admired the teacher, liked the work, received praises for neatness, tidiness and skill; and built up a picture of himself as a mature and acceptable member of the school group. Then one day in the playground there was some rough play by slightly older boys. Ted was knocked down. A child screamed. Ted struggled to his feet. At that moment the head of the school appeared, darted at Ted, shook him violently and scolded him publicly for roughness and bullying. "Not a credit to the school." "Disgraceful behaviour." Ted did not fully understand all that was said; but the whole setting of the incident concentrated his attention upon the remarks. His emotions were stirred; and his audible protest of innocence was insufficient to strengthen his self-respect against the subconscious reinforcement of the implication of failure and rejection. The statement was given weight by the prestige of the teacher who had made it; and in a generalised form it attached itself to all his school work. "Not a credit." He began to make blots, to stutter, to hesitate, to fail—where formerly he had succeeded. He became one of the pupils who do not fulfil their early promise; and the reprimands which followed served only to implant more firmly the suggestion of his incompetence.

All of these conditions of heightened attention, emotional reinforcement and prestige-value are present in competentlyhandled school situations; and therefore the educative potentialities of the relationship between teacher and taught are almost alarming in their strength. The whole subsequent life-story of a child may be modified by an admired teacher who implants the "suggestion" that he is a fool, a weakling or a failure; and similarly the redemption of an unhappy child may come through one teacher who believes in him—who succeeds by similar means in restoring the belief that hope is justifiable, and that ultimate recognition and acceptance will follow.

How may a teacher secure the prestige with a class which his office as an educator seems to demand? The answer to this question is closely bound up with the apparently different question as to what is involved in leadership.

A distinction has here to be made between a leader and a mere "headman". The superficial leadership consequent upon appointment to certain positions, or the possession of a certain measure of wealth or social rank, is not to be confused with the "leadership" which is genuinely worthy of the name. And in the intimacies of home or school or club, the externally applied labels of "parent", "teacher" or "leader" will avail little to the individual who tries to exercise leadership without cultivation of the qualities which make leadership possible.

Fortunately, the qualifications for leadership are neither unusual nor rare. The good teacher or leader has certain attributes of confidence, consistency, and justice. These can be cultivated through careful preparation and training, through self-criticism and also through the social maturing by which human beings escape from petty selfishnesses and absence of self-control. Leadership is also quite specific. It depends not merely upon the qualities of the leader, but upon the characteristics and expectations of the led. Most human beings are leaders in some circles.

The genesis or birth of leadership may be observed wherever human beings congregate. In very simple forms it can be noted among nursery school pupils, in playgrounds, in hotels, in camps or on board ship.[2] In all such social situations, the formation of small groups can be watched. The principles according to which groups are formed seem to depend not merely on similarities of age, of intelligence, of social background, of height, of past history, of geographical proximity, or identity of sex or race. (All of these possible elements have been investigated.) They may include any of these; but they also involve a certain "kinship" or community of interests and attitudes. And out of such groups, as he studies them, the observer may often note the emergence of a leader. Most frequently such a leader is one who shares the prevailing interest of the group—who possesses to a somewhat greater degree than the others, the qualities which make for "kinship" among its members, and who has (perhaps through awareness of his own skill or superior knowledge) a certain additional endowment of confidence and of expectation that his remarks will rise to the status of "suggestions", and win acceptance by the group who become his "followers" for the time being.

These characteristics of the genesis and the techniques of leadership serve as a guide to the young teacher who is trying to cultivate the qualities necessary to the successful educator. He requires to be essentially akin to the group among whom he hopes to find followers. He must share their interests and understand their needs—and this not merely verbally or superficially. The relationship is one at a level deeper than that of mere words. The judgments made by pupils as to the qualities of their so-called leaders take place through other media than words. "How can I hear what you are saying, when what you are is thundering in my ears?" He may also be comforted (or humbled) by the knowledge that it is unlikely that he will be equally successful with every group. The qualities of leadership are specific rather than general. They differ in different communities. The leader among athletes may not be a leader in a study circle. The teacher admired by one class may be less appreciated by another. If a teacher seems to fail with one group, he may prove more successful with another; and—an even more comforting thought—if his teaching appears uninteresting to-day upon one topic, it may prove more attractive on another occasion with another topic. His own confidence may be greater, his own enthusiasm may be deeper, and his personal appeal to the class may be stronger. Differences in such situations seem often to issue from quite trivial origins; and part of the interest of the educative process to the educator is associated with just this fact that he is dealing all the time with social relationships of extreme subtlety and sensitivity. It is dangerous to attempt to predict the exact effect of any specific attempt to commend a modification in behaviour, to advertise a new set of values, or to demonstrate a new form of skill to any given group, on any given occasion.

REFERENCES

1. cf. Brown, W., *Psychological Methods of Healing*. Univ. of London Press, 1938.
   Murphy, G., *et al.*, *Experimental Social Psychology*. Harper, 1937.
2. cf. Cowley, W. H., *Three Situations in the Study of Leaders*, "Journal of Abnormal and Social Psychology", XXIII, 1928, pp. 144–57.
   Buhler, C., *The Social Behavior of Children*, in *A Handbook of Child Psychology*, Murchison (ed.). Clark Univ. Press, 1933.

MURPHY, L. B., *Social Behavior and Child Personality.* Columbia Univ. Press, 1937.

PIGORS, P., *Leadership or Domination.* Harrap [n.d.].

PARTRIDGE, E. D., *The Social Psychology of Adolescence.* Prentice Hall, 1939.

SHERIF, M., and SHERIF, C. W., *Groups in Harmony and Tension.* Harper Brothers, 1953.

CARTWRIGHT, D., and ZANDER, A. (ed.), *Group Dynamics : Research and Theory.* Row, Peterson, 1953.

SHEARS, L. W., *The Dynamics of Leadership in Adolescent School Groups,* " Brit. J. Psychol.", XLIV, 3, pp. 232–42, 1953.

See also:

KLEIN, J., *The Study of Groups.* Routledge, 1956.

ARGYLE, M., *The Scientific Study of Human Behaviour.* Methuen, 1957.

CHAPTER VI

THE CHANGING OF BEHAVIOUR: GROUPS CAN MODIFY INDIVIDUALS

ARE there any comparable forms of influence exercised by groups in the attempt to educate individuals? This question follows naturally upon the one dealt with in the last chapter.

To a large extent it seems true to say that the "teaching" undertaken by groups is less deliberate than that attempted by individual parents or teachers. The social controls employed by brothers and sisters, acquaintances, companions and friends are, however, no less real on this account. They can be observed in simple forms among quite small children; and from the age of five or six onwards their structure and organisation are fairly well defined. The social situation again consists of two parts. It is not now a relationship between a dominant (or would-be dominant) individual who through prestige, leadership or attractiveness succeeds in raising his "instruction" to the status of an accepted "suggestion". The picture is rather that of a closed circle into which an outsider seeks an entry; and it is a recognised part of the situation that entrance is only afforded to outsiders to the degree to which they yield to the requirements of the group.

As has been noted above, one of the fundamental needs of human beings is security through acceptance by other individuals and by admired groups. This need for acceptance supplies the motive to which groups appeal in the techniques they use for the modification of individuals.

The requirements of membership are not always clearly formulated. They may consist of identity of family, school, or club, proximity of residence or similarity of age, sex, physique, interests, knowledge, dress, equipment and the like. "All of us live in Beacon Street. He is different. We want nothing to do with different people." And the Beacon Street children look the other way when he approaches. They attack him physically. They give him a nickname. They whisper about him, point at him, shout insults after him. He knows perfectly well that he is excluded; and he understands dimly that to secure admission he must do one of two things. He must either change his residence and come to live in Beacon Street, or he must contrive to secure sufficient prestige to render some other bond of kinship so attractive that he can disrupt the Beacon Street group and form a new group under his own influence.

A third possibility is of course open. He may decide that he is indifferent to the influence and the power of the Beacon Street group—that his loyalty and allegiance are in quite another circle—and he may therefore be unaffected by anything that the Beacon Street children may do or say. This state of indifference, it is to be noted, can be reached only if the individual concerned has had his need for the security of acceptance satisfied by affection and recognition received in some other circle. Further, if his indifference is genuine, the social pressure or petty persecution exercised by the Beacon Street group will soon cease to be sufficiently interesting to stimulate a continuance of their activities. A certain tension or responsiveness is necessary before such relationships can persist. A situation can be reached in which there is no further freshness or sense of adventure attached to the endeavour of the group to secure their new member.

Similar social controls can be observed in later age-groups; and, while the crudity of their expression seems to become progressively less, the mechanisms used are quite similar to those observable among little children.

Much of what used to be described as the "tone" of a school is maintained by these devices. Some of this "tone" is deliberately fostered by teachers; but, if the teachers do not succeed in acquiring sufficient prestige, the social pressure of small groups within the school often works against their wishes.

Physical violence, social slights and nicknames are the negative means employed by groups in their educating of individuals. The positive incentives are physical caresses, welcoming smiles, praise and pet-names. "Not one of us." "One of us." "We do this." "We don't do that." "Well done."

Similarly, within the class-room a large portion of what used to be called the "authority" of the teacher depends upon a teacher's skill in utilising the social pressure of the group to reinforce his wishes. Reward and punishment are largely effective as a result of their social meaning. Their power cannot be accounted for in terms of absolute value. A word of praise from one teacher may be of more effect than a bribe from another. The disapproval of a teacher who has been rejected may be a passport to acceptance by his pupils. (A record of conviction in a Juvenile Court may be the only accepted means of entrance to a certain gang.)

It is to be noted that there is no reason to believe in a mystical difference between the characteristics of a group and the characteristics of its members. The reactions of a group as a whole are essentially the same as those of the individuals who compose it. There is a certain increased sense of security attached to acceptance as a member and a consequent accession of courage. Pupils in rebellious groups may persecute teachers by means which they would not dare to employ alone; but they do no more than they each wish to do in the light of their previous relationships with teachers, and they follow gladly the suggestions made to them by their leaders only because of their awareness of their essential kinship with the point of view typified by the leader. The nature of this point of view is determined by their past history, their present intentions and their wishes for the future.[1]

This does not mean, however, that the point of view of a group, a gang or a mob cannot be changed. In any class there are always potential as well as actual outsiders, and a teacher's opportunities for leadership result partly from this fact. The group situation itself is also extremely open to modification. The character and the wishes of a group may at any time be changed by the addition of a new member. It may also be modified by the loss of a member. The whole pattern of class responses in a school-room may be altered by rearrangements in seating, in time table, or in opportunities for conversation. A problem child may secure a fresh start if unpropitious family groupings can be changed or if a new circle of friends can be found. Teachers and club-leaders have endless opportunities of experimenting with the curative possibilities of regrouping as well as of deliberately utilising the educative influences of all the social controls unwittingly exercised by groups.[2]

REFERENCES

1. A useful analysis of mob reactions in the extreme form of lynching is given in "*Social Learning and Imitation*", by N. E. MILLER and J. DOLLARD. (Yale Univ. Press, 1941.) The book as a whole is worthy of study from the point of view of the young teacher desirous of understanding the means by which social pressures are built up and broken down.
2. cf. ROGERS, C. R., *The Clinical Treatment of the Problem Child*, Houghton Mifflin, 1939, for an excellent account of the uses of camps, institutions and foster homes in the treatment of difficult children.

See also:

POLANSKY, N., LIPPITT, R., and REDL, F., *An Investigation of Behavioral Contagion in Groups*, "Human Relations", III, 4, pp. 319–48, 1950.

REDL, F., and WINEMAN, D., *Controls from Within*. The Free Press, 1952.

GROSSER, D., POLANSKY, N., and LIPPITT, R., *A Laboratory Study of Behavioral Contagion*, "Human Relations", IV, 2, pp. 115–42, 1951.

SHERIF, M. *An Outline of Social Psychology*. Harper Brothers, 1948. Revised edition, 1956.

CHAPTER VII

PROCESSES INVOLVED IN LEARNING

DISCUSSION of this topic is difficult, partly because its subject-matter is almost commensurate with life. Varieties of type in human learning are nearly as many as the varieties of human experience itself; and much of the apparent contradiction in conflicting interpretations is due to the fact that disputants are talking of somewhat differing forms of experience at different levels of difficulty. A brief historical digression may be useful here.

At the time when the chief interest of educators was directed towards the production of intellectual changes, and when the educator's task was still commonly held to be the making of correct impressions on the wax-like table of a pupil's mind, the processes involved in learning were believed to correspond quite closely to the " teaching steps " of preparation, presentation, association with other knowledge, generalisations based on this, and application in fresh situations. The pupil was thought of as a passive recipient; and the training of a teacher was directed almost exclusively towards the elaboration of the " methods " and " teaching devices " through which the " presentation of lessons " could be perfected.

At a slightly later date, experimentation with animals and the study of physiology directed attention to the obvious activity of the learner in the learning process. Observations were made of the behaviour of rats, cats, and other animals under controlled conditions. It was realised that the learning of a new route through a maze or a new method of unlatching a cage was unlikely to begin until motivated by some need, or stimulated by some incentive. It was noted that many movements seemed meaningless—mere " trial and error "—but that responses were only initiated as a sequel to stimuli of observable kinds. As a consequence, the emphasis in discussions of learning shifted to a consideration of the processes involved in the sequences of " stimulus—response " and the conditions accompanying the successful establishment of " bonds " or " connections ". There was a tendency to concentrate upon the characteristics of sensations rather than of thought; and attention was given almost exclusively to observable behaviour as viewed externally by an impersonal recorder.[1]

Contemporary with these researches into the mechanics of learning, it is possible to trace a continued interest in the nature of thought or reasoning. Dewey made a fresh analysis of the process of teaching in terms of an encouragement of problem-solving—stimulated by "felt wants"—and led the way to a rethinking of the issues involved in education, which resulted in proposals such as those popularised by the Dalton Plan, the Project Method and the Winnetka Technique.[2] At about the same time in England, Spearman gave a not dissimilar account of the nature of cognition, and this, in spite of the very specialised character of its terminology, has been associated with practical proposals of a very comparable nature.[3]

Experimentation of a more strictly psychological type was meanwhile, in the laboratories of Germany, tending towards an interpretation based on the characteristics of perception rather than of sensation. In 1912, for example, Wertheimer, a psychologist with the training of a physicist, drew attention to certain properties of visual illusions, and of the appearance of figures in motion. That which is "perceived" is not identical with that which is literally "seen" or presented to vision. What is "seen" may be a series of isolated photographs. What is perceived may be a person in motion. What is "seen" may be an incomplete circle, or two squares one inside the other. What is perceived may be a completed circle, a tunnel, a picture frame or a raised mound. Perception is in terms of a total pattern, a form or a "gestalt" (to use the German word). It varies according to expectations and intentions; and it changes with quite small alterations in the angle of the observer or the actual nature of the related impressions presented. Stimulated by these findings, extensive researches were undertaken into the behaviour of animals and human beings; and by about 1926, this fresh interpretation of the process of learning was being popularised under the general title of the "Gestalt" psychology.[4]

More recently, this has been further elaborated into what is now known as Field Psychology or Topological Psychology. In this, an attempt to describe in terms of relationships is proving illuminating in the discussion of learning problems which otherwise defy analysis.[5] (Its interpretations harmonise well with the explanations of human behaviour offered by clinical psychologists; and in the pages which follow an effort will be made to describe in non-technical terms the findings of both lines of approach.)

A very simple illustration may, at this point, be taken from the experiences of a pupil on arrival at a new school. On the first few occasions he may be guided by a friend from the entrance hall to the class-room. This experience is similar to that involved in mere "repetition" of a new formula or mere singing of a verse of a new hymn. It is unthinking and incohesive in structure. Its emphasis is on isolated impressions—along a corridor, round a corner, along another corridor, upstairs, round again, in at an open door. The corridors are not distinguished from one another in any particular fashion. The journeying is blind and lacking in insight. So long as a guide is available deliberate " learning " of the route does not begin. There are no motives for learning and many social reasons for remaining dependent. One morning, however, the friend may be absent and the correct route may have to be discovered unaided. All the corridors look exactly alike. Did he turn left or turn right? Did he go up this set of stairs? Did he then turn right or turn left? An attempt to find the room has to be made by a process which to an observer looks like mechanical " trial-and-error ". If the pupil walks far enough along corridors, climbs stairs and goes round corners he will ultimately reach the class-room door. (This is the procedure apparently adopted by many.) The journey seems long, and successful arrival remains a matter of chance; but there are certain satisfactions associated with correct behaviour and there are some incentives towards improvement. " Learning " cannot yet be said to have taken place. One day, however—perhaps through some chance remark—the new pupil may discover that the school is built round two square courtyards, and that his class-room is in the corner of the left-hand block. " Is it really so simple as that? " " How could I have had any difficulty! " The room falls into place as part of the total pattern. It becomes related to its own field—a part of the school as a whole. Insight has been achieved. Learning has taken place. A route once so learnt is not readily forgotten. Knowledge is now dependent not on mere repetition of stimuli, mere setting up of connections (" establishment of bonds ") or mere trial-and-error. The plan of the school is now understood. The corridors are no longer meaningless passages whose similarity is puzzling. They have become quite distinct routes—one shorter, another longer—and each with recognisable characteristics and distinguishing features. What is the relevance of all this to the teacher's problem when he is confronted with pupils whom he has undertaken to help to learn? The wording of the question is a pointer towards an answer. It is no longer believed that the chief responsibility of the teacher is to " teach ". The activity of the learner is recognised as a necessary element in the process, and the teacher's task is looked upon as that of a guide, an encourager, a leader, a diagnostician, rather than as that of an instructor, a ruler, or a law-giver.

When does learning take place? Why does learning take place? How does learning take place? These questions may be considered in turn.

Much learning occurs without very deliberate intention on the part of the learner. Much of it is of the nature of what is commonly called imitation. The social techniques of ordinary conversation, meal-time behaviour, shopping, travelling, etc., are absorbed almost unwittingly by children from the social circles in which they live. They are very often ignorant of the possibility of any other sort of behaviour; and the process of learning is probably as nearly effortless as any which can be studied.

On closer inspection, however, certain observations can be made. The learning, for example, of the techniques of eating is motivated very strongly by certain fundamental human needs—both physical and psychological. The child is hungry. He uses the quickest possible means of securing the food which satisfies that need. At first that is all he perceives in the situation. At a later stage, he discovers that admiration and approval follow certain sorts of behaviour and that "barriers" are erected against other ways of acting. These "barriers" may be psychological (in the form of disapproval) or physical (the removal of improper implements, or the use of punishment as a cue to the nature of what is frowned upon). The child wishes the approval of beloved adults and acceptance by his own social group; and, motivated by these needs, he tries again and again until the required behaviour is learnt. "We do not put our knives in our mouths." "We do not lick our plates." "We do not drink out of finger-bowls." To an adult accustomed to different conventions, the equipment of a hotel dinner-table may seem bewildering in its complexity. To a child who has grown up with such things, each implement has its meaning and its function.

It is to be noted, however, that the learning which on retrospect seems effortless has in fact been achieved by slow stages. In the first place, it was dependent on the physical and mental maturation of the child. That fact is usually recognised by those who superintend the learning of young babies. Until a certain degree of muscular control is achieved, it is useless to ask an infant to use a knife instead of a spoon. (At a certain stage, of course, he is obviously ready for neither.) It is customary to admit this, and to reward each small advance as it occurs, rather than to scold or to punish what looks like retardation. (Unfortunately at later stages the part played by maturation is more often forgotten; and pupils are ostracised for failure to perform actions which belong properly to a stage of maturity beyond that which they have reached.)

Secondly, the attempt to learn is often repeated. By its nature, the need for food occurs relatively frequently. Practice is in terms of minutes. Intervals between practice is in terms of a few hours.

Thirdly, the imitation of adult procedure is at first in quite a generalised form. Here is a spoon. Here is food. Adults do something about moving food with a spoon. The child imitates without fully particularising. The spoon goes towards the mouth, but it is upside down. At a later stage there comes a form of " insight " or what a recent writer has called " hind-sight ". A spoon can be used the other way up. If that is accomplished, various benefits follow. " Is that all there is in it ? " " Is it really as simple as that ? " The process of learning no longer looks like what may be described as " trial and error ". The child has matured sufficiently to understand, and the desired action is no longer too difficult for him to perform. He has reached the stage of " insight " into the function of the spoon. Thenceforward, progress will be rapid ; and, if adequate motivation is continued, his skill will mature steadily to the level of perfection which is desired by his social circle.

The function of the parent or teacher has been that of a guide, an encourager, an exemplar. His responsibility has been to study the situation as a whole—to supply incentives for learning, to strengthen the motives which initiated the process, to discover the reasons for apparent difficulties and delays, to ensure that too much is not attempted at any one time, to guard against undue disappointment and defeat, to grade the tasks so that the satisfactions of success may strengthen the budding confidence of the learner.

Quite comparable responsibilities fall upon the teacher charged with the organising of learning of more complicated forms of behaviour at later stages in growth ; and quite comparable stages in the recognition of meaning (or insight into functions and relationships) can be noted among pupils in other fields (such as those presented by widening vocabulary, by an understanding of number, by modifications of attitudes, changes in interests or alterations of values). Atomistic interpretations in terms of the consequences of mere repetition or drill, and mechanistic explanations on the lines of mere trial and error (with satisfactions somehow subsequently associated with " correct " responses to stimuli) are inadequate to account for the experience of insight enjoyed when the new thing to be learnt falls into place as part of a pattern of meaningful material.

" Learning " does not occur as a result of mere subjection to impressions. It is not sufficient that a pupil be present in a room in which chanting of number combinations may be heard (to take an example from the teaching of arithmetic). It is not even enough that he himself repeat audibly the " facts " which are to be reproduced. Memorising does not genuinely begin until he becomes active and for some motive (or because of some incentive) wishes to learn, and sets himelf to learn. Mastery does not show itself until he understands what is happening sufficiently to fit the number-combinations into their places as part of an organised and meaningful system of adding, multiplying, subtracting or dividing. Excellent service was rendered to the cause of good teaching by the emphasis on the analysing of subject-matter into component parts or " unit-skills " which followed upon Thorndike's description of the process of learning in terms of the establishment of correct " associations " or " bonds ". Step-by-step grading of material, diagnostic testing and remedial treatment based on the results of such testing have all become possible as a consequence of his work; but, from the learner's point of view, understanding remains a necessary preliminary to full conquest of a new skill.[6]

Similar illustrations of the importance of presenting material in a form in which " organising " or " recognition of relationships " is possible, may be taken from other school subjects. The beginnings of reading have been taught by schemes based on meticulous analysis into elements—alphabetic, phonic or phonetic. It has been found, however, that genuine learning does not commence until the pupil has reached a certain maturity, and has attained a sufficient vision of the whole to organise the material for himself; and experimentation with the apparently impossible procedure of beginning with entire sentences (meaningful wholes which make learning worth while) has shown that better working habits and greater ultimate skill result from such a type of presentation.[7]

In the teaching of foreign languages, of mathematics and of science, a comparable encouragement of activity and of understanding on the part of the pupil is taking the place of an emphasis on the thorough memorising of discrete elements.[8]

It has already been remarked that learning is practically coextensive with living. It is not merely a characteristic of the activities of childhood and youth. Acquisition of new forms of skill, memorising of new fields of knowledge and acceptance of new sets of values are processes which continue into adult life and old age. Their cessation is a sequel to deliberate intention and to absence of practice rather than a consequence of maturity.[9] It is never too late to learn; but learning is possible only if the would-be learner believes he can learn, wishes to learn and is prepared to take the necessary steps towards understanding, practising and perfecting the content of the modification (in his knowledge, his activity or his outlook) which he wishes to achieve —in order the better to satisfy his own fundamental needs of acceptance by the group, and of growth on lines approved by the group to which for the time being, in his own thinking, he belongs.

REFERENCES

1. For useful accounts of all this see—
BODE, B. H., *Conflicting Psychologies of Learning*. Harrap, 1929.
MURPHY, G., *An Historical Introduction to Modern Psychology*. Kegan Paul, 1929.
MURCHISON, C. (ed.), *Psychologies of 1930*. Clark Univ. Press, 1930.
Representative discussions are also given in——
THORNDIKE, E. L., *Educational Psychology*. Teachers' College, 1913.
WATSON, J. B., *Behaviorism*. Norton, 1924.
SANDIFORD, P., *Foundations of Educational Psychology*. Longmans Green, 1938.

2. cf. DEWEY, J., *How we Think*. Heath, 1910.
PARKHURST, H., *Education on the Dalton Plan*. Bell, 1922.
DEWEY, E., *The Dalton Laboratory Plan*. Dent, 1924.
KILPATRICK, W. H., *Foundations of Method*. The Macmillan Co., 1925.
WASHBURNE, C., *et al.*, *Results of Fitting Schools to Individuals*. Public School Publishing Co., 1926.
FLEMING, C. M., *Individual Work in Primary Schools*. Harrap, 1934.

3. cf. SPEARMAN, C., *The Nature of Intelligence and the Principles of Cognition*. Macmillan, 1923.
DUNCAN, J., *The Education of the Ordinary Child*. Nelson, 1942.

4. cf. KOFFKA, K., *The Growth of the Mind*. Kegan Paul, 1924.
KOHLER, W., *Gestalt Psychology*. Bell, 1930.

5. The most accessible discussion along these lines is probably that on *Environmental Forces*, by K. LEWIN in *A Handbook of Child Psychology*. Clark Univ. Press, 1933. This may be supplemented by Partridge's application to adolescent development of the concept of an object studied in relation to its field (Partridge, *loc. cit.*), and by HARTMANN, G. W., *Gestalt Psychology*. Ronald Press, 1935. An excellent comparison of the interpretations of connectionists, bond-psychologists, gestalt psychologists and field psychologists is given in *The Psychology of Learning*. Forty-first Yearbook of the National Society for the Study of Education, Part II. Public School Publishing Company, 1942.
See also ;
HILGARD, E. R., *Theories of Learning*, Appleton-Century-Crofts, 1948.
SMITH, F. V. *The Explanation of Human Behaviour*, Constable and Company, 1951 and 1960.
POFFENBERGER, A. T., *Modern Learning Theory*, Appleton-Century-Crofts, 1954.
THORPE, L. P., and SCHMULLER, A. M., *Contemporary Theories of Learning with Applications to Education and Psychology*, Ronald Press, 1954.
ALLPORT, F. H., *Theories of Perception and the Concept of Structure*, John Wiley, 1955.
HARRIS, T. L., and SCHWAHN, W. E., *Selected Readings on the Learning Process*. Oxford Univ. Press, 1961.

6. cf. THORNDIKE, E. L., *The Psychology of Arithmetic*. The Macmillan Co., 1922.
BALLARD, P. B., *Teaching the Essentials of Arithmetic*. Univ. of London Press, 1928.

BRUECKNER, L. J., *Diagnostic and Remedial Teaching in Arithmetic.* John C. Winston, 1930.

BUSWELL, G. T., BROWNELL, W, A., *et. al.*, *Research in Arithmetic.* Twenty-ninth Yearbook of the National Society for the Study of Education, Part II. Public School Publishing Co., 1930.

These may be contrasted with—

Arithmetic in General Education. Sixteenth Yearbook of the National Council of Teachers of Mathematics. Teachers' College, 1941.

Interesting experimental work with numbers—

KATONA, G., *Organising and Memorising.* Columbia Univ. Press, 1940.

See also:

WERTHEIMER, M., *Productive Thinking*, Harper Brothers, 1945.

STERN, C., *Children Discover Arithmetic*, Harper Brothers, 1949.

BUSWELL, G. T., BROWNWELL, W. A., *et al. The Teaching of Arithmetic*, Fiftieth Yearbook of the National Society for the Study of Education, Part II, 1951.

For a general summary reference may be made to

FLEMING, C. M., *Teaching: A Psychological Analysis.* Methuen and John Wiley, 1958.

7. cf. Fleming, C. M., *Individual Work in Primary Schools.* Harrap, 1934.

For a summary of researches see—

FLEMING, C. M., *Research and the Basic Curriculum.* Univ. of London Press, 1946 and 1952.

See also:

STRANG, R., MCCULLOUGH, C. M., and TRAXLER, A. E., *Problems in the Improvement of Reading.* McGraw-Hill, 1946 and 1955.

RUSSELL, D. H., *Children Learn to Read.* Ginn and Co., 1949 and 1961.

GATES, A. I., *Reading in the Elementary School*, Forty-eighth Yearbook of the National Society for the Study of Education, Part II, 1949.

GRAY, W. S., *The Teaching of Reading and Writing: An International Survey.* UNESCO, 1956.

Fleming, C. M., *Teaching: A Psychological Analysis.* Methuen and John Wiley, 1958.

8. cf. HAMLEY, H. R., *Relational and Functional Thinking in Mathematics.* Ninth Yearbook of the National Council of Teachers of Mathematics. Teachers College, 1934.

9. cf. THORNDIKE, E. L., *et al.*, *Adult Learning.* The Macmillan Co., 1928.

BRUNER, J. S., *The Process of Education.* Harvard Univ. Press, 1960.

SKINNER, B. F., *Cumulative Record.* Appleton-Century-Crofts, 1961.

PART II

PUPILS BELONG TO MANY GROUPS

CHAPTER VIII

FAMILY INFLUENCES

PUPILS belong to many groups. All these groups exercise some degree of formative influence; but many of them are inevitably outside the school. A teacher who wishes to understand his pupils must therefore look beyond the class-room and try to study the other communities which also form part of the field in which the youngsters are developing.

The first in time-sequence of a child's extra-school experiences is the home into which he is born. It is desirable to discover as much as possible about the family, the parents, and the influence, if any, which a pupil's position in the family-group exerts upon his observable characteristics.

Contact with the home is not always easy to effect—especially in schools of a residential type. It is, however, very well worth attempting. Some knowledge of family circumstances may alter significantly the attitude both of teacher and pupil. A restless twelve-year-old may, for example, cease to seem annoying when it is known that he has no time for play because he has to help in his father's shop both before and after school (and a teacher who has shown genuine interest in that fact may unwittingly be accepted as a friend whose expectations it is desirable to fulfil). An adolescent who is embarrassingly friendly may be more fully understood when it is realised that he is an orphan who lives with somewhat unresponsive guardians. A bully may be more readily helped towards social adjustment when it is known that there is severe quarrelling at home, that he takes his absent father's side and that his mother, while giving him no share in family responsibilities, shows marked preferences for younger brothers and sisters. Frustrations of the basic human needs of adventure, of affection, of recognition, and of responsibility have their effect upon behaviour in school as well as at home; and partial satisfactions in school compensate, to some extent, for deficiencies at home. Increased co-operation between school and family, especially through discussion of common problems in Parent-Teacher Associations, has been proved to result in greater happiness and effectiveness in both communities.

In such discussions certain significant problems emerge. How far are the characteristics of pupils—in intellectual activities, practical skills or social interests—determined by the qualities of their parents? "Mary is just like her father. I can do nothing with her." "Margaret's mother was convicted of theft. What can be expected of her?" "Jim's father can't spell. He will never do any better." "Elsie's mother was mentally defective. She is not worth teaching." "Jack's father is a skilled mechanic. He should be one also." "Maud's home is very poor. Too much must not be expected of her."

The likeness of children to parents is not a discovery of educational psychology. It has provided a theoretical justification for caste distinctions and class distinctions for more centuries than are recorded. It has been used as an argument for excluding entrance to certain professions and as an excuse for compulsory shepherding of sons into their fathers' occupations. Children have been threatened with the temperamental fate of their fathers and (less often) they have been encouraged to believe in their own potentialities as members of superior groups.

The topic is closely associated with philosophic discussions of the relative parts played by inheritance and environment; and it may be noted that emphasis has varied broadly from century to century (with the prevailing political and social sympathies of the disputants) from a conviction that inherited qualities are unmodifiable and all-important (that the "education" of certain groups is probably not worth attempting) to a belief that obvious inequalities in performance are entirely to be explained by differences in environment (in "education").

Within the last few decades efforts have been made to study such questions more objectively in the light of investigations and of controlled measurements. Theorising has been tempered by efforts to interpret evidence obtained from studies of the ancestry of feeble-minded persons or of men of genius, of the offspring of parents known to be mentally defective or brilliant, and of the resemblances of fraternal and identical twins (on the side of heredity). Careful statistical analyses have also been made of records of the geographical distribution of men of science, of parental occupation in its relation to intelligence, of the resemblances of foster children to their foster homes, and of the measurable consequences of unstimulating treatment (as indications of the part played by environment).

These studies have been supplemented in other fields by work, for example, on the science of genetics [1] which now emphasises the diversities of germ-cells in each parent and the extent of the possible variations in the combination of genes. This diversity (and the fact that inheritance is biparental) serves in some measure to explain differences among children of the same parents as well as dissimilarities between parents and children. The fact that the germ-cells within each parent are not entirely disparate seems associated with the existence of some degree of correspondence between brothers and sisters and between parents and children. Such findings accord very well with the present position of psychological research which recognises the limits set by original endowment although it is now much more sensitive than formerly to the amount of variability within sub-groups of families and friends.

Earlier formulations of the problem (in terms, for example, of "Heredity and Environment: Their Influence on Intelligence" or "Nature and Nurture: Their Influence on Achievement") are of relatively little interest to educators since it has to be admitted that it is difficult, if not impossible, to distinguish rigidly between what is hereditary and what is environmental. The concern of teachers is also less with the discovery of the content of innate endowment than with the understanding of intelligent behaviour (of any type) when it appears among their pupils. They, therefore, ask evidence on the observable resemblances (correspondences [2] or "correlations") between parents and children or teachers and pupils: and they are very willing to co-operate in experimental study of the demonstrable effects of changes in environment. A brief summary of relevant work seems desirable here.

Intellectual resemblances within families have been estimated from studies of the ancestry of the feeble-minded and of men of genius as well as by comparisons of parents and their children. About 80 per cent. of feeblemindedness has been attributed to inheritance; and the degree of correspondence ("correlation") between the measurable intelligence of mid-parent and child has been reported to range from $+ 0{\cdot}3$ to $+ 0{\cdot}6$ with an average of $+ 0{\cdot}5$.[3]

A correlation of this size does not, of course, imply that all mentally defective children are born of mentally defective parents. (Complete correspondence would be represented by a correlation-coefficient of 1.) It indicates a certain degree of relationship; but it leaves room for considerable variation. Studies of the children of mothers known to be mentally defective (whose fathers were believed to be also of low-grade intelligence) support the expectation [4] that the measured intelligence of children may differ somewhat from that of their parents. Comparable findings emerge from the study of brilliant children; and correlations between the intelligence of brothers and sisters show degrees of resemblances which increase from about $+ 0{\cdot}5$ to about $+ 0{\cdot}9$ with the closeness of the relationship.[5] These do not exclude the possibility that the closer degree of resemblance between fraternal twins (+ 0·7) than between ordinary brothers or sisters (+ 0·5) may be attributable to greater identity of the environment in which they are reared; and they do not indicate that the intelligence of a pupil may be confidently estimated from the known intellectual level of his parents (or even of his brothers and sisters). The child of a mentally defective parent may prove to be quite "worth teaching". Elsie will not necessarily be "just her mother over again".

Comparable studies of resemblances within families have been attempted in relation to obvious behaviour-problems like delinquency; and from the results of these also there seems reason to believe that all delinquents do not come of criminal ancestry [6] and that the children of delinquents will not inevitably prove guilty of indictable offences. Margaret will not necessarily follow her mother into petty pilfering. Given wise treatment, there is every reason to hope for better behaviour from her.

Parent-child relationships with regard to emotional dispositions and temperamental traits are more difficult to assess and they have been less frequently studied. There seems little doubt however, that maladjusted parents have maladjusted children. Emotional abnormalities among children are apparently the result of unpropitious circumstances operating upon handicapped children from homes whose emotional atmosphere is unwholesome. The findings of studies of delinquency are again of interest in this connection. On the whole the evidence is that children showing delinquent tendencies come from unwholesome homes and that their emotional maladjustments are accompanied by emotional maladjustments on the part of the parents.

Other intrinsic characteristics of the home such as attitudes and loyalties can be estimated more readily since they are more frequently expressed in verbal form; and within the last few decades much attention has been given to techniques for their measurement. There seems reason to believe that pupils' opinions on matters connected with the family, the school, the Church, industry and the State are more closely related to those of their parents (+ 0·6) than to those of their teachers (+ 0·12).[7] The highest correlations are also found between the judgments of parents and children (+ 0·54) on matters involving ethical discrimination. These are closely followed by those between intimate friends (+ 0·35) while club leaders, day-school teachers, and Sunday School teachers seem to exercise progressively less influence (+ 0·137, + 0·028, + 0·002) as their relationship becomes more remote.[8] These experiments were carried out with paper-and-pencil tests inviting judgments on stories embodying situations such as: "Jean's family were too poor to buy fruit for her sick brother, and every now and then she took an orange from the fruit stall and brought it home to him." Opinions on such issues do not necessarily correspond to conduct. (Convicts and teachers have been known to express quite comparable views.) The results of various studies seem, however, to indicate that pupils have differing codes for different environments; and that prestige, intimacy and duration of contact are crucial in their effect upon opinions and behaviour.

Relationships within families in attitudes towards the Church, towards war and towards communism also show correlations of about $+0{\cdot}5$. There is a certain similarity; but there are differences between children in the same home which seem to be related to differences in treatment by the parents as well as to variations in extra-familial experiences (and appear to change when these are modified).[9]

The cumulative evidence of investigations into attitudes (as into behaviour and intelligence) is, therefore, favourable to the belief that it is not unreasonable to hope for family variations from parental patterns. Children are not necessarily ineducable because they come from homes where the level of performance seems low. Mary and Jim are not bound to be just like their fathers.

This leads to a consideration of a further question: To what extent can the influence of the parents (whether it is environmental or hereditary in its working) be counteracted by other forces?

Some evidence on this question is given by reports on the results of treatment of problem children referred to guidance clinics and other such agencies.[10] There seems reason to believe that the earlier that modifications are made in an unsuitable environment the more likely is success to be obtained, and that character is definitely modifiable. Experimental evidence in support of this belief is offered by Voelker[11] who tested the overt behaviour of six groups of boys of ages ten to fourteen (matched for performance on an initial test). Two of the groups received training with deliberate emphasis on honesty—in addition to regular scout training—while two groups received scout training, and two other groups had no deliberate teaching of any kind. After seven weeks it was found on a retest that most progress had been made by those receiving deliberate training, and least by those with no training at all. While the number of cases does not justify definite conclusions and the time-interval was short, the study does suggest that measurable conduct is susceptible to educational influences.

Confirmation of a more general kind is also given by many studies of personality traits in their interaction with differing situations.[12] Personality is re-defined from one situation to another. Personality traits in pre-school children show marked changes in altered social settings. Behaviour varies strikingly in accordance with the personality of those with whom older children come in contact. Sympathy-responses change dramatically with variations in security as well as with other modifications in the total situation. Delinquents treated as "bad" girls and "bad" women remain measurably and predictably "bad"; but when they are treated as human beings, they behave as such.

The possibility of such beneficial effects of changes in environment is at present, perhaps, more readily accepted in relation to conduct than to intellectual ability. The findings of research that there is some degree of constancy of the average I.Q. of groups on retesting as well as evidence of some correlation between the intelligence of parents and children have led teachers to believe that nothing can be done for the intellectually dull but that their intellectual level is fixed at birth.

Certain research findings on measurable changes in the intelligence of children who have been removed from the influence of their own parents (whether through death or some other cause) are important in this connection. These seem to show a significant degree of correlation between mental development and the quality of the foster home (+ 0·48). Brothers and sisters reared [13] in significantly different homes show less resemblance (+ 0·25) than that ordinarily found with sibs reared in the same home (+ 0·5); and the claim has been made that the maximal effect of the best home environment may be to raise the I.Q. twenty points. (This finding is the more impressive since it occurs in a discussion which attributes to heredity about 80 per cent. of the variance in intelligence).[14]

From reports such as these it has been concluded that changes in environment can change intellectual performance and that in this case also, the sooner the change occurs the greater its effect.

The frustrating effect of poor social and intellectual conditions seems also indicated by studies of the children of gypsies and canal-boat workers and certain isolated mountain communities in which steady mental deterioration and decrease in I.Q. appear to occur with advancing age.[15] It has, however, to be noted that there is a considerable degree of unreliability in the testing of such children, and that intellectual poverty in the home probably accompanies a low level of parental intelligence.

Studies of environmental effects are incomplete without some attempt to assess the degree to which intellectual performance is related to other characteristics of the home such as socio-economic level, or material possessions. Sweeping statements have sometimes been made to the effect that of course the brighter children come from the more prosperous homes; and teachers have often been tempted to advise against continuance of secondary education because of a low level of parental income. While poverty does result in a dangerous lowering of the level of nutrition, there is, in this connection also, reason to believe that the variations which occur from home to home are related to intrinsic characteristics such as attitude and point of view rather than to extrinsic attributes such as prosperity or possessions. When homes are classified according to the occupational level of the parents (or according to any other purely socio-economic criterion) it is found that many dull children come from the A group and many bright children from the groups classified as C or D.[16]

The average of children's intelligence does, on the whole, appear to rise with the occupational level of the parents; but the overlapping between one grade and the next is so great (and the size of the sub-groups differs so much) that, while socially superior parents produce a relatively larger number of children of higher ability, mediocre homes [17] produce an absolutely larger number. Correlations between the intelligence (or achievement) of children and their socio-economic level are positive but not high. They approximate to $+ 0{\cdot}3$ according to most reports. This is not surprising in view of the low degree of correspondence which is known to exist between intelligence and income. (The most acquisitive are not always the most intelligent.)

Some understanding of the importance of the intrinsic characteristics of the home is reflected in other questions which are also asked in Parent-Teacher Conferences. "Meg's father is dead. Has she any chance of developing well?" "Bill is an only child. Is he sure to be spoilt?" "Beth is the baby of the family. How can she become independent?" "Alec has a stepmother. What can you expect?"

The most propitious family influences are commonly believed to be those found in a normal family; and it is therefore not surprising that there have been recurrent attempts to estimate the degree of association between broken homes and misdemeanours of various kinds.

It is to be noted, however, that many studies confuse the issue by combining data for broken and for badly-supervised homes; and unexpectedly negative findings have resulted from careful analysis of the mere completeness of the family of delinquent boys in comparison with that of other boys of the same age, race, nationality and district. The incidence of homes which have been actually broken is not always significantly higher among delinquents; and the inference seems to be that a formal break in the home is a less serious factor than internal discord and tension in family life. The loss of a father may be less harmful than the ill effect of an unsatisfactory one.

Some findings have been reported as to the accompaniments of various other types of incompleteness in the family circle. Illegitimate children have been said to be characterised by bad physical development and inefficiency in school. Step-children are often neglected and distrustful; and institution children may be intellectually retarded as well as emotionally starved.[18]

Evidence, on the whole, however, seems to indicate that the objective fact of living with both parents is in itself of less consequence than the child's emotional relation with his parents, the degree to which he feels accepted and beloved, and the extent of harmony and co-operativeness within the family circle. Foster children are not alone in suffering from uncertainty. Step-children are not alone distrustful. Inefficiency at school and inferior physical development are not confined to illegitimate children. Orphans are not the only group whose questions may remain unanswered and who may suffer from an undesirable number of commands and an undesirable absence of parental affection.

A comparable emphasis on the importance of intrinsic rather than extrinsic characteristics results from a consideration of the observable effects of ordinal position in a family.

This has been studied in great detail—at first in relation to obvious conditions such as feeble-mindedness, disease, or delinquency, and later in connection with assessments made through standardised tests of intelligence, of school achievement, or of attitude.[19] (The expectation was that birth order would be paralleled by an ascending or descending order of social conformity, of health or of intelligence; and it was assumed that the conclusions reached could be used in discussions of the "trend of the race" and as a means of stimulating parents to more eugenic practices.)

Very conflicting evidence has been obtained; and most of the studies of complete families (with careful matching according to parental age, number of children, neighbourhood, sex and nationality) indicate that this absence of clear-cut distinction is due to the complexity of the inter-relationships among brothers and sisters. It is not necessarily true that the eldest is sure to be brilliant or dominant, that the youngest will be dependent, or that the only child will be spoilt, unhappy, conceited or sickly. Characteristics seem to be related to the attitudes of the parents and to inter-familial experiences of rejection or favouritism,[20] rather than to order of birth or even to differences of sex.

The same appears to be true of children's attitudes to their parents. Self-sufficient children are predominantly antagonistic to both mother and father; while preferences for either parent seem to be related to the treatment given by the parents, rather than to the sex of the parent or the child.

REFERENCES

1. cf. JENNINGS, H. S., *The Biological Basis of Human Nature.* Norton & Co., 1930.

2. These correspondences have been studied by statistical methods. Useful summaries of investigations are given in—
   TERMAN, L. M., *et al.*, *Nature and Nurture: Their Influence upon Intelligence*; and *Nature and Nurture: Their Influence upon Achievement.* Twenty-seventh Yearbook of the National Society for the Study of Education, Parts I and II. Public School Publishing Co., 1928.
   FREEMAN, F. S., *Individual Differences.* Harrap, 1934.
   STODDARD, G. D., *et al.*, *Intelligence: Its Nature and Nurture.* Thirty-ninth Yearbook of the National Society for the Study of Education, Parts I and II. 1940.

3. cf. LEAHY, A. M., *Nature—Nurture and Intelligence.* Genetic Psychology Monographs, 1935, pp. 235–308.
   See also CONRAD, H. S., and JONES, H. E., *A Second Study of Familial Resemblance in Intelligence.* Thirty-ninth Yearbook, *loc. cit.*, *II*, pp. 97–141.

4. See STODDARD, G. D., and WELLMAN, B. L., *Environment and the I. Q.* Thirty-ninth Yearbook, I, *loc. cit.*, pp. 405–42.
   VERNON, P. E., *Intelligence and Attainment Tests.* Univ. of London Press, 1960.

5. cf. TERMAN, L. M., *Genetic Studies of Genius.* Stanford Univ. Press, 1925 and 1930.
   WINGFIELD, A. H., and SANDIFORD, P., *Twins and Orphans*, "Journal of Educational Psychology", 19, 1928, pp. 410–23.
   See also CARTER, H. D., *Ten Years of Research on Twins.* Thirty-ninth Yearbook, *loc. cit.*, I, Ch. VIII.

6. cf. BURT, C., *The Young Delinquent.* Univ. of London Press, 1925.
   GLUECK, S., and GLUECK, E. T., *One Thousand Juvenile Delinquents.* Harvard Univ. Press, 1934.
   GLUECK, S. and E., *Unraveling Juvenile Delinquency.* Commonwealth Fund, 1950.
   STOTT, D. H., *Saving Children from Delinquency.* Univ. of London Press, Ltd., 1952.

7. SMITH, M. M., *Comparative Social Attitudes*, "Journal of Educational Psychology", 28, 1937, pp. 681–93.
   For discussions of techniques for measuring attitudes see—
   VERNON, P. E., *Personality Tests and Assessments.* Methuen, 1953.
   REMMERS, H. H., *Introduction to Opinion and Attitude Measurement.* Harper Brothers, 1954.
   BREWSTER SMITH, M., BRUNER, J. S., and WHITE, R. W., *Opinions and Personality.* John Wiley, 1956.

8. HARTSHORNE, H., and MAY, M. A., *Studies in the Nature of Character.* The Macmillan Co., 1928–30.
   See also PECK, R. F., and HAVIGHURST, R. J., *The Psychology of Character Development.* John Wiley, 1960.

9. cf. MURPHY, G., *et al.*, *Experimental Social Psychology.* Harper, 1937.

10. cf. EISSLER, K. R., *Searchlights on Delinquency.* Imago Publishing Co., 1949.
POWERS, E., and WITMER, H., *An Experiment in the Prevention of Delinquency.* Columbia Univ. Press. 1951.
11. VOELKER, P. F., *The Function of Ideals and Attitudes in Social Education.* Teachers' College, 1921.
12. *v.* MURPHY, G., *et al., loc. cit.*
WATSON, GOODWIN (ed.), *Civilian Morale.* Houghton Mifflin, 1942; and
LEWIN, K., *et al., Patterns of Aggressive Behavior in Experimentally-created "Social Climates",* "Journal of Social Psychology", 10, 1939, pp. 271–99.
13. *v.* FREEMAN, F. N., *et al., The Influence of the Environment on the Intelligence, School Achievement and Conduct of Foster Children.* Twenty-seventh Yearbook I, *loc. cit.*, pp. 102–217.
14. *v.* BURKS, B. S., *The Relative Influence of Nature and Nurture upon Mental Development.* Twenty-seventh Yearbook, I, *loc. cit.*, pp. 219–316.
Cf. FREEMAN, F. S., *loc. cit.*
STODDARD, G. D., and WELLMAN, B. L., Thirty-ninth Yearbook, I, *loc. cit.*, and criticism by GOODENOUGH, F. L., and by TERMAN, L. M. Thirty-ninth Yearbook, I, Ch. XI and XIV.
15. cf. FREEMAN, F. S., *loc. cit.*, and Goodenough, F. L., *loc. cit.*
16. cf. LAWRENCE, E. M., *An Investigation into the Relation between Intelligence and Inheritance,* "British Journal of Psychology Monographs". 1931.
17. A summary is given in LOEVINGER, J., *Intelligence as related to Socio-Economic Factors.* Thirty-ninth Yearbook, *loc. cit.*
See also HAGGERTY, M. E., and NASH, H. B., *Mental Capacity of Children and Paternal Occupation,* "Journal of Educational Psychology", XV, 1924, pp. 559–72.
FLEMING, C. M., *Socio-Economic Level and Test Performance,* "British Journal of Educational Psychology", XIII, II, 1943, pp. 74–82.
FLOUD, J. E., *et al., Social Class and Educational Opportunity.* Heinemann, 1957.
18. ORLANSKY, H., *Infant Care and Personality,* "Psychol. Bull.", 1–48, 1949.
PINNEAU, S. R., *The Infantile Disorders of Hospitalism and Anaclitic Depression,* "Psychol. Bull.", 52, 5, pp. 429–52, 1955.
BOWLBY, J., *et al., The Effects of Mother-Child Separation: a follow-up study,* "B. J. Med. Psychol.", XXIX, 3 and 4, pp. 211–247, 1956.
19. For good summaries of work on birth order see—
JONES, H. E., *Order of Birth,* in MURCHISON, C. (ed.), *A Handbook of Child Psychology.* Clark Univ. Press, 1933; and
MURPHY, G., *et al., loc. cit.*
20. KROUT, M. H., *Typical Behavior Patterns in Twenty-six Ordinal Positions,* "Journal of Genetic Psychology", 55, 1939, pp. 3–30.
See also BOSSARD, J. H. S., and BOLL, E. S., *Family Situations.* Univ. of Pennsylvania Press, 1953.
SCHACHTER, S., *The Psychology of Affiliation.* Tavistock Publications, 1961.

CHAPTER IX

COMMUNITY INFLUENCES

THE influence of extra-familial groups has been indirectly indicated by the summary of research given in Chapter VIII. This evidence does not mean that other community agencies have no importance; but where parents have succeeded in establishing prestige and maintaining intimate contact, the modifications directly attributable to other groups outside the family are much fewer than where parental leadership is weak. They are also unlikely to be in a direction opposed to that favoured by the traditions of the home.

In this connection the influence exerted by the group is of a slightly different type from that discussed in Chapter VI. The techniques here used are those employed by a group to retain a member within its influence. "We do not do that." "We do this." "You will be an outsider if you do that." "We shall not admire you any more." "You are one of us. You could not possibly do that." And, if the child is happy within the family circle and proud of his position in it, he decides to conform—in order to retain his picture of himself as a member of the home.

The first situation in which the issue arises is often that of the formation of street groups to play the games of early childhood. At this point many later social patterns are outlined. If a parent thinks of children as possessions—toys, things to play with, objects to be kept clean and to be reserved for oneself—an attempt is usually made to keep the child within the nest and to prevent outside contamination. Opposition is offered to the establishment of free contact with other groups. (This may be supported by strong opinions as to the inferiority, the "rudeness" and the "roughness" of most other children in the district.) Fear of society is a frequent consequence of such treatment, and along with this fear may go a sense of isolation and of loneliness induced by looking out through cage-bars at the apparently happy group-activities of the "others". Comparable unhappiness may be caused by the parents who think of children as young animals to be trained to obedience—"puppies", "whelps"—or as young savages whose destructive and aggressive impulses require constant prohibitions and threats. The child of such parents is less able to fit harmoniously into social groups outside. He expects opposition and is prepared to rebel, or he anticipates bullying and is characterised by quarrelsome resentment. This resentment is in turn reacted against by other children and they come to expect the same type of behaviour-pattern to be shown on every occasion. It very often is—until a different sort of treatment produces [1] a change in the social attitude of the child.

The actual nature of the influence exerted by a street group depends not only on the past history of the children who compose it but also on the nature of the activities open to them. Observable behaviour therefore differs in town and country, in suburban districts and in the crowded streets of a great city. In certain places, the only possible adventures involve interference with traffic or the "collection" of objects from "Woolworth's". In such places (for those whose parents do not effectively erect barriers of disapproval) the chief entertainments are teasing the policeman and petty pilfering of a variety of types. For other more fortunate children the activities favoured are those approved by larger groups of adults. They therefore escape being labelled as "young delinquents".[2] Their needs are satisfied in more acceptable fashions. They also, however, have come under the sway of community influences.

Obvious differences between types of play activities and of leisure pursuits in town and country have led to expectations of marked differences in performances in school as well as in attitudes towards learning. Reliable evidence is somewhat scanty—partly because of the differences in the training, qualification and status of teachers and partly because of the difficulty of securing representative samples of pupils in the districts where these differences are greatest. When testing has been rigorous and where differences in teacher personnel are small, there seems, however, reason to believe that residence in the country is not accompanied by measurable decreases in response to schooling or in performance in intelligence tests. In a survey in Scotland of all children born in a given year, it was found, for example, that the percentage of pupils with low scores from rural or sparsely populated areas did not differ significantly from that of pupils in urban or densely populated areas and the same conclusions held for pupils with high scores.[3]

Similar differences in communal behaviour are reported in most studies of the evacuation of city children to billets in the country. The interpretation of such evidence is again difficult because of the effect upon evacuees of emotional distress, separation from home, unwilling entrance into new groups and the like. The issue is further complicated by changes in their level of nutrition and the possible influence of such changes on the nature of preferred activities and on observable temperament and attitude towards life. These responses in turn are associated with the relationship of the evacuees to the standards and the wishes of the communities they have left.

Such community influences are to a large degree involuntary

and unwitting. More deliberate influence is exerted on slightly older groups by the instruction attempted by adult workers through media such as Sunday Schools, the organising of games, the opening of play centres, and the establishment of clubs of various kinds. Membership of such groups undoubtedly produces some effect [4]; but little has yet been done to assess its nature or estimate its degree. Many pupils are known to maintain almost complete independence of formal groups.[5]

Less obvious community agencies operate through broadcasting, the cinema, libraries and art galleries, concerts and the silent instruction given by advertisement hoardings. Much has been written on these influences but relatively little evidence has yet been obtained by means of controlled experimentation and objective testing.[6]

Certain observations may, however, be made.

The effect of residence in a particular locality makes itself felt in various ways. The most obvious is probably that of the physical conditioning consequent on different types of housing. In the overcrowded streets of a great city,[7] pupils suffer from lack of space in which to keep their possessions, lack of privacy for their own adventures, and absence of opportunities for exploration of the properties of earth, air and water. Their behaviour in school is affected by this; and wise schooling makes some attempt to allow for such deficiencies. At the same time it has to be noted that compensatory devices are already operating outside the school. Some houses are such as to "drive one to the Pictures twice a week". But in the Picture-House companionship can be found. (The lonely are admitted into the sharing of a group-experience.) There is privacy in warm and sheltering darkness, along with adventures of various kinds and a certain definite status and recognition as a seat-holder whose seat has been paid for. In the selection of a picture-house also, for the most part, there are opportunities for the exercise of independent judgment and initiative; and, if the range of choice be small, there is at least the right of criticism and the satisfaction which follows from that activity. A Picture-House audience may seem to a casual observer to be gullible or lacking in understanding and taste. Closer study reveals very definite standards of judgment and quite clearly formulated desires. (Their expression may not be in the terms employed by literary critics in University circles.) These wishes are related partly to the physical conditions under which the community lives. They therefore vary from district to district with differences in the size of house available, the amount of garden space, and the opportunities for creative activities of other kinds. They are also affected by the nature of the work done by adult groups and the varying degrees of physical exhaustion and differing levels of nutrition consequent upon this. The monotony and relative loneliness of a repetitive job seem to increase the craving for rapid movement, contact with large numbers of people and observation of colour and pageantry. The fatigue associated with such work is also often so great that the mere passivity of spectatorship is all that is consciously desired. Professional or business men and women resident in the same district may ask for entirely different forms of communal activity.

It is to be noted that these characteristics of the life of the adult community determine the nature of what reaches the children. Community influences find expression through the attitudes of relatively small groups of friends who meet regularly in face-to-face contacts. Children hear the remarks of their elders and make their choices along lines acceptable to the group whose opinion they value most highly. The reactions of a number of such small groups determine to some extent the type of " picture " or play offered in any district. They also produce observable variations in the sort of programme which proves popular and in the measurable effects of such a programme on the knowledge and the attitudes of young people.[8]

It is possible to collect statistics showing the distribution of cinemas, clubs, or public-houses, the area of hoarding used for advertisements, or the approximate numbers of listeners to specified broadcasts. (Careful community surveys can also be made on the lines of those published in England for Tyneside, Merseyside, London or York.)[9] Even such detailed studies do not, however, permit exact estimation of the degree of influence exerted by each community agency. There is a sense in which it seems true to say that attendance at a cinema is " a habit rather than an interest ". It is possible to " see " many advertisements without " noticing " any. It is possible to " hear " the loudspeaker without " listening " to the broadcast. It is not unusual to " look " at television and " perceive " very little. (There is indeed some reason to believe that the amount remembered may be in inverse relation to the amount so experienced.) Learning is not a mere consequence of subjection to impressions; and, without conscious understanding and critical activity on the part of the pupil, the effect of the multiplicity of urban agencies may amount to little more than an awareness that there are many things to be seen and many sounds to be heard.

In this connection also it may be noted that even within one locality there are wide individual variations. These differences (as in the case of the other family influences mentioned in the last chapter) depend on the intrinsic rather than the extrinsic characteristics of the home.

There are certain groups who " never go to the Pictures ", " do not listen to the wireless ", " are not members of a library ", " do not go to Church ", and so on; and, for the most part, the children (as was noted above) conform more closely to the patterns of these intimate circles than to those of more remote groups outside.

There are many homes in which entertaining activities are carried on under external conditions which might have been expected to make family life an impossibility. There are many schools in poor localities whose teachers are wise enough to share in the adult activities of the neighbourhood. Such teachers and such parents may become sufficiently vital in outlook to be able to provide satisfactions for the children's need of variety, of change, of adventure; and such homes and such schools (even in the most unpropitious external surroundings) can lead to that delight in present activity which develops at later stages into enjoyment of work of any kind and a wholesome width of interests and independence of vision.

In relation to all these factors, it can be remarked (as was noted above in connection with the leadership exercised by individuals upon groups) that a community's response to deliberate attempts to influence it or to instruct it may take the form of apparent indifference or of deliberate rejection. The most palatial buildings and the finest equipment will not, for example, buy popularity for clubs, schools or libraries unless they are conducted in fashions which satisfy the ordinary human needs of security and adventure and make provision for the exercising of sufficient responsibility in activities arduous enough to be both interesting and stimulating.

This is a sufficient reason for cautious scepticism about the charges sometimes brought against mechanised entertainments as a " cause " of delinquency, of inattentiveness, or of inability to work. It is doubtful whether there is much difference in content between the appeal of a ballad-monger's tale in a feudal castle, a " penny dreadful " under the desk in a Victorian school and a thrilling film in a present-day cinema. They deal with major human issues such as " love, faith and courage "—to quote a recent advertisement—but not all who see nor all who hear desire to imitate. Not all accept the educative influences offered; and incitement to delinquent behaviour is more often found in defective personal relationships and social maladjustments than in mere knowledge of possible activities or proximity of usable opportunities.

Excessive looking at television may lead to eye-strain, to interference with sleep, to diminished exercise in the open air, or to an undue expectation that all stories will have a happy ending. Other activities may have quite comparable consequences. Inattentiveness in school and inability to concentrate are known to be also directly associated with malnutrition, poor ventilation and a lack of experience of the satisfactions of concentrated endeavour. Frustration and interference with chosen activities in childhood lead to diminution in willingness to persevere; and morale in schools as well as in workshops is directly related both to previous success and to the knowledge that achievement is possible.[10] The extent of such knowledge is itself a somewhat imponderable but not insignificant form of community influence.

REFERENCES

1. cf. SAYLES, M. B., *The Problem Child at Home.* Commonwealth Fund, 1928.
   RADKE, M. J., *The Relation of Parental Authority to Children's Behavior and Attitudes.* Univ. of Minnesota Press, 1946.
   CUNNINGHAM, R., *et al., Understanding Group Behavior of Boys and Girls.* Teachers College, Columbia University, 1951.
2. Excellent discussions on delinquency are given in books such as—
   HEALEY, W., and BRONNER, A. F., *New Light on Delinquency and its Treatment.* Yale Univ. Press, 1936.
   ROGERS, C. R., *The Clinical Treatment of the Problem Child.* Houghton Mifflin, 1939.
   BRILL, J. G., and PAYNE, E. G., *The Adolescent Court and Crime Prevention.* Pitman, 1938.
   Making Citizens. H.M.S.O., 1945.
   GITTINS, J., *Approved School Boys.* H.M.S.O., 1952.
3. cf. RUSK, R. R., in HAMLEY, H. R. (ed.), *The Testing of Intelligence.* Evans, 1935.
4. MACALISTER BREW, J., *Youth and Youth Groups.* Faber, 1957.
5. For a discussion of the techniques of the use of such group membership as a means of treatment see ROGERS, C. R., *loc. cit.*
6. For accessible summaries of evidence see—
   CRONBACH, L. J. *Educational Psychology.* Harcourt, Brace, 1954.
7. cf. SHAW, C. R., and MCKAY, H. D., *Juvenile Delinquency and Urban Areas.* Univ. of Chicago Press, 1942.
8. On films see the studies financed by the Payne Fund in America.
   HIMMELWEIT, H. T., *et al., Television and the Child.* Oxford University Press, 1958.
9. See also BARKER, R. G., and WRIGHT, H. F., *One Boy's Day.* Harper Brothers, 1951.
   OESER, O. A., and HAMMOND, S. B. (ed.), *Social Structure and Personality in a City.* Routledge and Kegan Paul, 1954.
10. cf. WATSON, G. (ed.), *Civilian Morale*, Houghton Mifflin, 1942, for evidence of the improvement in industrial output consequent on the introduction of limited goals and knowledge of progress.

CHAPTER X

SCHOOL INFLUENCES

NEXT to the home, the school seems to exercise the greatest influence on child life. Intimacy of relationship, considerable prestige and regularity of contact contribute to this; and also the fact that its opportunities for producing modifications extend over a period of nine to thirteen years. Most pupils do not, however, at present come to school in the first five years of life; and, except in orphanages, the educational supervision of the school is not continuous.

What is the effect upon learning of membership of a school group?

Its effect upon measurable achievement has been very thoroughly studied in the last few decades. Results obtained by experimentation are not, however, easy to interpret. There are, for example, very many psychological functions which may be taken as testing material.[1] There is a wide range of differences in age, intelligence, schooling and attitudes among pupils. There are variations in the possible size of groups, and variations in the relationship between members of the group.

On the whole, the effect of co-workers is stimulating; but the social increment seems greater for those of low intellect than for those of high and also more for slow workers than for swift workers. It also varies with the social attitudes of individuals; and is, for example, less for stutterers than for those whose speech is normal. Its direction is determined by the nature of the subject-matter. Work on material which is to be reproduced individually seems more speedy but less accurate under group conditions; but group discussions (of the type of committee-work or work on a jury) can produce a more complete and accurate account of details than can the record of an average member. The presence of others seems also to lead to more objective thinking—with greater fluency but a poorer quality of ideas.

The effect of spectators varies both with the individuals and with the type of occupation in which they engage. Written work under close supervision tends to be less accurate but more rapid; and there is some evidence that activities involving manipulative dexterity show a retardation in rate when watched.

The effect of competition upon performance is similar to this. For the most part it results in more work, but work of poorer quality. Awareness of success produces an improvement in score; and the effect both of rivalry and of knowledge of success is more obvious with slower and duller workers.

Co-operative learning produces better social adjustment for both superior and inferior pupils. The effect of praise or encouragement is greater than that of reproof; but both are more effective than the absence of any such motivation. Similar findings attach to the use of stronger cues such as reward or punishment. (This seems independent of age and level of ability. It is probably related to the individual's need for recognition—either adverse or favourable—and it varies with social relationships within the group.) Reproof leads to a sudden spurt, but progressively loses its effectiveness. Encouragement results in a confidence and stability which facilitate a continuance of learning.

The consequences of the social relationships of the class-room are further complicated by the varying effects produced by differing attitudes towards teachers and differing types of handling by different teachers. It is well known to all members of school groups that behaviour depends not merely on the composition of the group but on the fear, respect, affection, indifference or hostility aroused by the personal characteristics of the teacher and the assessment made thereon by the class. This assessment may be quite mistaken; but, until it is modified, it exercises a definite influence.

An important early study of the effect of teachers' attitudes was made some years ago by means of a questionnaire [2] devised to discover the relationship between child-behaviour and the expectations and point of view of teachers. It was found that individual teachers had specific patterns of reported behaviour in their classes. Some had classes who were (according to the teachers) almost all aggressive, talkative, dishonest, indecent, careless, untidy. Others had classes composed of friendly, co-operative, diligent, and willing pupils. The discrepancies were so great that it seemed unlikely that they corresponded to differences in actual pupil-characteristics. It was also found that the verdicts of different teachers on children's misdemeanours did not agree; and that teachers as a group ranked as most serious any offence against the code of silent and submissive behaviour supposed to characterise the "perfect pupil" in a docile class. (This was probably associated with the faith in repressive discipline associated with over-emphasis on the hereditary, fixed and aggressive character of instinctive behaviour and the accompanying belief in the need for control through fear and severity.)

Comparable evidence of a more impersonal kind has been

obtained by the use of objective recording of pupils' responses and by cinematograph reproductions of their actions and expressive gestures.[3]

Behaviour has been shown to be a function not merely of the character of the pupil but of the treatment given by the teacher and the school. Authoritative and dictatorial handling produced aggressiveness towards weaker members along with an absence of responsibility when compulsion was removed. Neglect resulted in discouragement and depression. The fostering of co-operative activity led to joyful release of energy and happy diligence.

The same children responded differently to different types of treatment. Under autocratic leadership they followed instructions submissively enough (especially if they had not experienced a less repressive form of discipline); but they worked only when watched and showed little initiative and an absence of co-operative friendliness. Their manner and gestures indicated apathy and some degree of boredom; and the venom aroused by the handling they received showed itself in petty persecution and tale-bearing directed against one another. As soon as the teacher left the room, the group disintegrated and work ceased. Under *laissez-faire* discipline there was a restless boredom of a slightly different type. The pupils seemed to suffer from the lack of definite goals and the absence of an understanding of their objectives. Morale was low; and irresponsible horseplay was not infrequent. Under democratic discipline the manner of the class changed. Gestures and facial expressions altered. The pupils became more alert and seemed more competent. Petty persecution ceased. Dependence on the teacher became progressively less; and work was carried through with considerable initiative even when immediate supervision ceased.

Transition from one type of response to another took a little time. The democratic leader who followed an autocrat had to exercise patience before his whole group adjusted themselves to the new conditions. But readjustment did take place. The autocratic ruler found his task more difficult if his class had known a more mature type of handling; but if he was unscrupulous enough he could produce superficial submissiveness of a more or less temporary kind. The pupils adjusted themselves to the total situation under each variety of educative influence. They did not show fixed, unalterable, and consistent behaviour patterns (whose origin might usefully have been ascribed to unlearnt instincts whose strength was peculiar to each pupil as an individual). Their reactions rather indicated that behaviour as a whole changes when its meaning is modified. Actions that were impossible in one context were readily learnt and willingly performed in another.

These observations in this connection may seem so obviously true as scarcely to merit recording. Their significance in relation to future experiments in the re-education of human beings is greater than can at present be realised.

All of these findings are very relevant to a study of the possibility of educative modification of behaviour as well as to an analysis of the means through which such modifications may be achieved. They help to account for the measured success of school methods which endeavour to adapt instruction to the needs, interests and abilities of the pupils and seek to produce socialised behaviour by opportunities for co-operative endeavour on what is conveniently called " Individual Work ".

There are much stronger grounds now than formerly for a belief in human educability. Much has still to be discovered as to the best stimuli to use ; but the evidence already secured (both through experimentation on lines inspired by a Gestalt or Field Psychology and through clinical records) indicates the consequences of skilfully directed re-education in the spheres of conduct, of attitudes, and of school achievement, as well as in the growth of what is commonly called intelligence. (A useful analogy may be taken from comparable developments in the science of nutrition.[4] There is now much more reason also for a belief in the possibility of modifications in human energy, abilities and attitudes through skilfully directed nourishment given at suitable periods. Much has still to be discovered about the limits set by inherited characteristics ; but the evidence already obtained—both through experimentation with vitamins and through clinical records of the consequences of such experimenting—is sufficient to justify a much greater expectation of change than seemed at one time possible.)

It is never too late to learn ; and learning is a constant accompaniment of human experience. Flexibility and the power to adjust to varying circumstances characterise all human beings ; and the agencies through which such modifications are fostered are as varied as the groupings in which human beings find themselves from day to day.

REFERENCES

1. For useful summaries see—
   MURPHY, G., *et al.*, *Experimental Social Psychology*. Harper, 1937.
   cf. also DASHIELL, J. F., in MURCHISON, C. (ed.), *A Handbook of Social Psychology*. Clark Univ. Press, 1935.
   SPROTT, W. J. H., *Social Psychology*. Methuen, 1952.
2. cf. WICKMAN, E. K. *Children's Behavior and Teachers' Attitudes*. Commonwealth Fund, 1928.

3. cf. LEWIN, K., *et al.*, *Patterns of Aggressive Behavior in Experimentally created " Social Climates "*, " Journal of Social Psychology ", 10, 11, 1939, pp. 271–99.
   WATSON, G., *Civilian Morale*. Houghton Mifflin, 1942.
   See also ANDERSON, H. H., *et al.*, *Studies of Teachers' Classroom Personalities*. Applied Psychology Monographs of the American Psychological Association, 6, 8, 11, 1945 and 1946.
   OESER, O. A. (ed.), *Teacher, Pupil and Task*. Tavistock Publications, 1955.
4. cf. ORR, J. B., *Nutrition and Psychology*, " Journal of Education ", 75, 885, 1943.
   For a general survey see:
   FLEMING, C. M., *Teaching: A Psychological Analysis*. Methuen and John Wiley, 1958.

CHAPTER XI

INDIVIDUALS WITHIN GROUPS

AT this point a return may be made to the subject-matter of Chapters I and II. Within the last few decades very great developments have occurred in the accuracy with which both intelligence and personal characteristics can be assessed. It is now possible for a skilled observer, using test material whose validity and reliability have been established, to obtain information as to present performance much more fairly and accurately in an hour or two than he could have done formerly in many months with the unstandardised methods of ordinary class-room or family contacts.

This increased skill in diagnosis has had two consequences. It has led to a much greater awareness of the extent of individual differences; but it has tempted teachers, parents and administrators to behave as if the measured relative positions of pupils were quite fixed. Teachers and administrators now know that children differ widely in intelligence, skill, interests and maturity. They have, however, been too apt to assume that these differences in their present form will be lasting—that tests have great predictive as well as diagnostic value.

The practical consequences of these two deductions have probably not yet fully appeared.

Awareness of the range of individual differences within a group of pupils in any class-room (as within any wider grouping such as that of sex, of age, of socio-economic level, of country or of race) has resulted in the demand for adaptation of instruction to their needs. This is a relatively recent phenomenon; and methods by which the necessary flexibility and teaching skill may be developed are still being worked out.[1] The necessity for such adaptability on the part of the school and the home is, however, quite generally admitted.

Accompanying this, there very often goes the implicit assumption that (in spite of any teaching skill shown) those pupils whose measurable performance at a given age is poor will remain at a lower level throughout their career. This has resulted in a dangerous emphasis on the usefulness of selection and classification as contrasted with tuition and educational guidance. There has been greater willingness to accept defeat—to assume that certain groups are inherently " stupid ", " sickly ", " bad ", " unsuitable "—than to experiment into the results of a different type of teaching, a different sort of nutrition or a new variety of social relationship. The fixity of initial characteristics and innate impulses has been emphasised rather than the educability of any human organism within the limits set by an inheritance whose potentialities are as yet only imperfectly understood.

The subject is sufficiently important to merit further consideration. The sequence has been something like this. Psychologists were invited to assist in prediction. They devised test material and evolved methods of determining its validity and reliability. They tested pupils. A few months (or years) later they re-tested the same pupils. They calculated the average I.Q. of the group on the first occasion and its average I.Q. on the second occasion; and certain of them made the remark that there was, as they had hoped, a considerable degree of "constancy" in the I.Q. "Speaking roughly, 50 per cent. of the I.Q.'s found at a later test may be expected to fall within the range between six points up and four points down. . . . It is evident, therefore, that the I.Q. is sufficiently constant to make it a practical and serviceable basis for mental classification."[2]

The observation was acceptable to teachers, administrators and parents. It was repeated without the expressed reservation and without a realisation of the degree of variability implied by such a modifying clause. Competent psychologists continued to experiment, and repeated the finding in general terms with similar conditioning phrases. Correlations for groups were worked out and proved positive and high. A belief in the "constancy of the I.Q." passed into popular speech; and on it was reared a whole edifice of school classification and organisation. The bright little boy, it was confidently expected, would become the bright senior. (It was even implied by some writers that the early-matur ng infant would become the brilliant older child.) The I.Q. was thought of as constant. Prediction of future relative intellectual status was believed to be quite possible. Administrators and organisers therefore began ever more confidently to assert that selection of pupils suitable for specific educational destinations could conveniently be made at about the age of eleven. Separation into educational streams proceeded merrily. The chief task for the future was considered to be the perfecting of the means of such segregation. (That is still the belief in very many quarters.)

Meanwhile, investigations were continuing. It began to be noted that rather surprising changes in averages occurred in certain social groups. It was reported, for example, that younger canal-boat children had an average I.Q. of about 90 at a mean age of five years and ten months while older children in the same families had an average I.Q. of approximately 60. Similar findings came from testing of groups of Kentucky mountain children and from the testing of mill-workers' children in a North Carolina town. An interesting converse to such studies was found in records of increases in I.Q. which seemed to correspond to continued residence in improved environments.*

These observations threw psychologists back on to a consideration of individual cases where the I.Q. had not remained constant; and research workers began to draw attention not only to the relative stability of the averages but to the range of individual change which was co-existent with a fairly stable average or a fairly high correlation of test with re-test. It was noted that changes of as much as twenty points in I.Q. did occur and that the size of the correlations decreased with the length of the interval between test and re-test—(dropping from something like $r + 0{\cdot}8$ for intervals below two years to approximately $r + 0{\cdot}6$ for intervals of five to twelve years). It was also observed that, even in a stable environment, there was evidence that the direction of the change seemed to bear some relation to the age at which the initial testing was done and to the initial intellectual level of the testee.[3]

Interest then turned to the observable results of the re-testing of larger groups of children at frequent intervals. Long-term studies of growth over a period of years were begun in Europe and in America. The results of such studies are only now becoming available. The findings of one of the most notable of these may be summarised as follows; [4]

Physical and mental growth seems characterised by cycles. Variability rather than consistency is the rule. Prediction, except for averages of groups, is extremely hazardous, and even that is hazardous during the period of adolescence. Growth is essentially an individual affair. The chronological (or physiological) age at which acceleration will occur is a function of the life-history of the individual. Size of any kind at any one age is not a prediction of size at any later stage. If, however, groups are selected on the basis of performance at any given age, a certain regularity of fluctuation in the growth rhythm may be detected. There is a tendency for all groups to regress towards the mean. While, in general, children remain in the same broad classification above or below the mean throughout their period of growth, the composition of any group is at the same time subject to fluctuation; and individuals may make surprising changes upward or downward. Each person follows a different path in relation to the yearly averages of the group as a whole.

It seems fair to interpret these findings as indicating that selection and classification of pupils at a given age is more dangerous than has been generally supposed. Realisation of the uni-

* Cf. Chapter VIII above.

versality of individual differences was a consequence of research undertaken at the opening of the century. Belief in the constancy of the I.Q. characterised the third decade. Recognition of the extent of individual variability in rate of growth is now emerging as a result of the surveys reported by psychologists since then.

This conclusion when formulated is not altogether unexpected. It serves to illumine certain observations which lie within the experience of most teachers and administrators.

Exact prediction has much more rarely been expected from measurements of physique than from estimates of intelligence or assessments of behaviour. It is, for example, not generally assumed that the child who is small or sickly at eleven will inevitably prove a puny adult. It is rather realised that better diet or wiser treatment may, within wide limits, transform such a child into an adult of normal or even of superior health. It is not commonly taken for granted that a petty thief at the age of eleven will mature into a hardened criminal at twenty-one. The evidence of observable variations in development seems accepted in both moral and physical spheres much more readily than it appears to be acceptable in relation to intelligence or educability.

It is quite a common complaint among educators that many children are "admitted" to secondary education who do not prove "suitable". This is frequently attributed to the present weaknesses of the instruments of selection. It may prove to be, in part at least, a consequence of human variability in rate and in incidence of growth.

It is also generally realised by enlightened teachers and administrators that a pupil may not "do himself justice" in an examination on any one day. That likewise may prove to be a result not so much of his unrepresentative performance on that one day as of the observable fact that prediction is more possible in relation to the individual's position in his own growth cycle than it is in relation to the group averages in terms of which results of testing are commonly expressed. (His own growth cycle can be estimated only in terms of objective and standardised measurements over a period of years. That implies observation and testing by highly trained teachers under the guidance of experts.)

The age of occurrence of the physical maturing which we call the onset of puberty is known to vary within wide limits—from about eight or nine to about eighteen or nineteen years. It is not so generally realised that evidence is accumulating which seems to indicate that there are also great variations in the age at which marked increments of mental growth occur.

Teachers know well from experience that rearrangement of pupils in the course of a session is frequently necessary in those schools where classes have been organised on the basis of homogeneous grouping. (This is one of the reasons why the attempt to group according to mental age has been abandoned in many districts after prolonged experimentation.) Such variability of attainment in different school subjects may prove to be not merely the result of variations in teaching methods, in attendance, in social satisfactions or in emotional health. It may also be a function of the ordinary variability in growth and maturing of which we are only now (as a result of long-term studies of large groups) beginning to collect evidence.

It may be useful here to notice the comparable developments which have occurred in the field of industrial psychology. In connection with education in industry, a consideration of the simpler issues of selection and classification also preceded work on the more complex problems involved in guidance. Careers-masters were at first a mere addition to the staff of a school. Tests were applied only at the end of a school career. Their results exerted no influence on curriculum or teaching methods. This stage was followed by a realisation that more useful evidence could be obtained from a confidential card on which might be recorded, over a period of years, observations as to personal characteristics, interests and activities—as well as the results of standardised tests in what is commonly called intelligence or school achievement.[5]

This is now being followed by a third stage in which it is increasingly realised that guidance, to be effective, must be continuous, that diagnostic testing should be followed by remedial work based on the evidence obtained by tests, and that marked modifications are necessary in curriculum and methods of instruction if training is genuinely to be adapted to the characteristics and the needs of human beings.[6]

REFERENCES

1. An accessible account of experimental work associated with this is given in—
FLEMING, C. M., *Individual Work in Primary Schools*. Harrap, 1934.
2. TERMAN, L. M., *The Intelligence of School Children*, p. 148. Harrap, 1921.
3. cf. NEFF, W. S., *Socio-Economic Level and Intelligence*, "Psychological Bulletin", 1938, 35.
PHILLIPS, G. E., *The Constancy of the Intelligence Quotient in Subnormal Children*. Melbourne University Press, 1940.
CLARKE, A. D. B., and CLARKE, A. M., *How Constant is the I.Q.?*, "The Lancet", 6791, CCLXV, pp. 877–80, 1953.
4. DEARBORN, W. F., *et al.*, *Predicting the Child's Development*. Sci.-Art Publishers, 1941.

With this may be compared:
MacFarlane, J. W., Allen, L., and Honzik, M. L., *A Developmental Study of the Behavior Problems of Normal Children between 21 months and 14 years.* Univ. of California Press, 1954.
Sontag, L. W., *et al., Mental Growth and Personality Development.* Child Development Publications, XXIII, 68, 2, 1958.
For discussion of educational implications see
Fleming, C. M., *Adolescence; Its Social Psychology.* London: Routledge and Kegan Paul, 1948, 1955 and 1963.
See also:
Clarke, A. M., and Clarke, A. D. B., *Mental Deficiency.* Methuen, 1959.
See also:
Fleming, *Teaching: A Psychological Analysis.* Methuen and John Wiley, 1958.

5. Cf. Oakley, C. A., and MacRae, A., *A Handbook of Vocational Guidance.* Univ. of London Press, 1937.
6. For interesting elaborations of this point of view, publications of the Progressive Education Association may be consulted—e.g.—
Thayer, V. T., *et al., Re-organizing Secondary Education.* D. Appleton Century, 1940.
cf. also Hamley, H. R., *Educational Guidance of the School Child.* Evans [n.d.].
Dennis, W., *Current Trends in Industrial Psychology.* Univ. of Pittsburg Press, 1949.
Rodger, A., *et al., Vocational Guidance and Training in Chambers' Encyclopaedia.* Newnes, 1960.
Fleming, C. M., *Teaching the Elements of Mathematics.* Ginn, 1961.

PART III

TEACHERS ARE ALSO PERSONS

CHAPTER XII

DEVELOPMENT

LEADERSHIP of a group is possible only on the part of individuals who share the characteristic interests and fundamental needs forming the bond of kinship which unites the group. Teachers can be leaders because they are first of all persons who have quite recently passed through the same stages as the pupils whom they teach.

It may be useful here to review very briefly the sequence of personal development as it appears in the life-history of most human beings. Any description can be, of necessity, only in the most general terms, since there are differences in physiological age at birth and observable differences in intellectual and social age even in the first few months of life.

Roughly speaking, the first year is characterised by extreme dependence, by satisfactions of a sensuous kind and by a love-interest which centres on mother (and on father to the degree to which he shares in the intimate contacts of feeding, washing and nursing). Expressive sounds and movements seem to arise chiefly as indications of the need for the satisfactions of food, warmth or sleep or in response to caresses symbolising love. There is very little evidence of awareness of other children or of desire for the approbation of anyone except the attendant parents (or parent-substitutes). Tenderness is exhibited, and admiring affection is obviously enjoyed. Anything which can be called anxiety is manifested only when unaccustomed neglect is experienced.[1] Behaviour which looks like fear occurs as a sequel to what may be interpreted as assault—unexpected noises or the sudden approach of loud-voiced strangers. What appears to be anger seems associated with frustration of the need for food or with interference in exploratory occupations. During these months many of the patterns of later emotional life are initiated ; and the foundations of mental as well as of physical health are laid. The extreme dependence of the infant gives especial importance to the behaviour of the one or two adults who determine his emotional atmosphere. The baby has no means of escape from the terrors of anxiety or insecurity if these are forced upon him by capricious, irregular, irritable or rough treatment. The child who is handled with tenderness, surrounded with affection, approached gently and fed regularly seems to experience neither fear nor anger; and, since he is practically indifferent to strangers, he begins to build up undisturbed the inner security, confidence and independence which characterise emotional health in adult life.

In the second year, life becomes more complicated. Movements cover a wider range. Exploration extends beyond the limits of the hearthrug or the bed. Crawling, standing, walking and running follow in rapid succession, and communication with other human beings begins to take the form of comprehensible sounds of socially acceptable patterns. Expressive cries and movements now indicate the need for more than nourishment and nursing; and awareness of social disapproval begins to manifest itself. Frustration by adults and temper-tantrums in response to such frustrations become more frequent as the variety of activities increases. Children can now move about, touch things, break things, damage things; and there is a danger that an increasing number of prohibitions may lead to the development of anxiety, distress and guilty fears. Alternatively there is a risk that the child may discover that through exhibitions of anger he can tyrannise over adults in the family circle.

The normal characteristic of the year seems one of adventure —explorations into the corners of the room, into cupboards, into the properties of toys, into the mysteries of feeding oneself, and into all the joys of the growing independence of the toddler who is preparing for the astonishing growth of the next period. At the same time the dependence of the first year is continued. There is the same need for continual reassurance and for a haven of protection to which to return. Awareness of other children and of visiting adults begins to show itself; and, where fears have not been implanted by unwise handling, the foundations of social confidence begin visibly to be laid. It is important that encouragement be given to the joyous adventurer. Precious possessions of adults can be moved to higher shelves so that the delights of exploration need not be interrupted, and parents can share in the child's maturing ability to play.

The third and fourth years are characterised by very rapid progress. Speech becomes not only comprehensible but articulate, fluent and complicated in structure.[2] Muscular skill increases and social sensitivity becomes almost distressingly acute. Children are now obviously aware of the thoughts and feelings of those whom they meet. Deliberate imitation becomes more frequent; and identification with the moods of beloved adults shows itself in reflected joy or sorrow. It becomes increasingly desirable that contact be made with a variety of human types; but it remains important (as through all the formative years) that the adults be serene, stable and emotionally mature—not given to frequent regressions into temper-tantrums, sulking, irritability, or unreasoning fear.

After the second birthday, many children are so well developed that social sanctions begin to be necessary. "This is mine. That is yours." "Do not touch mine." "We object if you touch ours." "We do not do that. We do this." For the fortunate child the number of mere prohibitions is still small, and the number of approved activities is very great; but a beginning can be made in the commendation of respect for property, of gentleness and co-operative play. This is achieved not chiefly through words but through the treatment given to the child. He has possessions of his own. His possessions are respected. He has opportunities of constructive adventure in activities of all sorts in co-operation with adults and other children. He has a hammer, a dust-pan, a brush, paper, paint, a share in a garden, a knife, scissors, a needle, a saw—according to the interest of the moment. And almost insensibly, through experiencing socialised living, he adapts himself to society and becomes able to take his place with the others in his circle—at a level of emotional maturity imitative of that which has been reached by its members. Experimentation into the social uses of temper-tantrums may still appear as an expression of growing independence; but if his world remains a stable one in which nothing is gained by crying and in which sulkiness brings no reward, the frequency of such experiments steadily decreases.

In these years from two to four a sense of what may be described as responsibility already shows itself. A younger baby may have appeared. Possessions are treasured and collected. Muscular control and activity develop sufficiently for the child to be able to run towards (and run away from) other children and adults who visit the family circle. (Fortunate children have such visitors coming into the home because their parents have outside interests of various kinds. Solitary children in many districts are able to make contact with one another in nursery schools.) The formation of small groups of two or three children begins to be noticeable. Preferences are expressed for certain playmates. Exploratory talking becomes increasingly articulate; and before the fourth birthday the stage of tireless questioning has usually been reached. Why? What? How? It is important that the child's need for recognition be met by treating this questioning with respect and extending to him the ordinary courtesies of mature social intercourse. If the apparently trivial questions of this stage are answered in friendly fashion without mockery or contempt, the later more profound problems as to the origins of life and the nature of the universe will suffer little morbid suppression or concealment.

Acceptance, adventure, and increasing independence—these needs characterise the pre-school child. They are met by the love of parents, contact with small groups of adults and children, opportunities for learning and experience of responsibility suited to the level of maturity he has reached. Regression into the anxieties of insecurity, into temper-tantrums, over-dependence, or timidity become less frequent in proportion as the child develops in social maturity.[3]

About the age of five years many children go to school for the first time. This extends very considerably the range of their choice of friends. Their love-interest widens to include a third important adult—the teacher; and their conversation and imitative play take on fresh forms. Slightly larger groups of girls and boys co-operate in simple group games; but grouping is still very fluid and there is little deliberate organising of activity. The healthy child shows increasing independence and conquers much of the routine of ordinary living—dressing, washing, feeding, serving food, travelling to school, tidying after play, helping in the home, simple shopping, reading and counting. "I can do it my own nice self" is a characteristic remark at this stage—indicative of adequate satisfactions of the basic human needs. There is a consciousness of power and a delight in exploring the world beyond the confines of the home or the street. Investigation into the properties of earth and water (through miniature digging and trenching in the garden, the gutter or the sand-pit) provides absorbing occupation for many hours. An increasing sense of responsibility is shown by the care of younger children as well as in the collecting of possessions. An interest in listening to stories is quickly followed by a discovery of the delights of story-telling; and through sharp-witted observation of the behaviour of adults the child begins to draw distinctions between fact and fiction, truthfulness and the telling of lies. The pattern he accepts is modelled closely upon the practice of the adults whom he admires. "How can I hear what you are saying when what you are is thundering in my ears!"

In contrast to the astonishing growth of the first four or five years, the life of the school child is much less interesting to ordinary adult observers; and, possibly because of this, the doings and sayings of the older girl or boy seem to play a much smaller part in the conversation of parents as well as in the records of students of child life. The baby has been adored. The toddler has been tiresome but still admired. The schoolboy comes and goes. He is busy with lessons and games. He does not change much in size or appearance and the years slip past with little apparent history. He still requires love, acceptance, recognition, adventures in learning and some share in the responsibilities of living. All these he receives in a home which is "good" and, in slightly different forms, in a school which is "good". And in proportion as he receives these he grows towards wholesome confidence, mastery of life and emotional and intellectual maturity.

This increasing independence is not a matter for regret, but is rather an indication that the child's development is proceeding on normal lines and that the adults who determine the emotional pattern of his life are themselves reasonably mature.

Psychological weaning can much more readily be achieved by parents or teachers who have wide and varied interests and occupations which carry their own thoughts away from a possessive concentration on every detail of the life of the school-child. Problem behaviour of one kind or another characterises the boy who continues to receive treatment more suited to infancy.[4]

Healthy mental and physical growth comes almost imperceptibly to the child who receives adequate nourishment—physical and intellectual—in an atmosphere of trust and serenity and against a background of orderly living. During these middle years a fortunate child builds up some knowledge of the virtues of truthfulness, honesty, cleanliness and decent conformity to customs of various kinds—as these are interpreted by the group of adults and children who form society as he knows it. He also acquires the essential skills of reading, writing and counting; and learns habits of concentrated endeavour which make possible the later conquest of more difficult forms of learning.[5] The inner confidence and security which accompany a reasonable measure of success in such activities serve to fortify his courage in the subsequent years of transition from childhood to manhood.

The period commonly called adolescence coincides with this period of transition—measurable roughly from the onset of puberty to the time of recognition by society as an independent and responsible adult. There is a very wide range of individual differences in the age at which the growth spurt occurs, and a corresponding danger in making any generalisations based upon mere age-averages.* There are also very great differences in

* Many of the earlier reports on the characteristics of adolescents give a somewhat misleading impression of steadiness of development and uniformity of type. Studies published more recently take account of the variations in individual attributes over a period of years; and educators are now much more aware both of the dangers of attempts at prediction and of the degree of overlapping between one group and another.[6]

the degree of social pressure brought to bear on young people and the nature of the complicated activities expected from those who attain adult status. The simpler the structure of society the easier seem the experiences of adolescents.[7]

During adolescence there comes to the youngster an increasing awareness of himself as an individual—a member of a group but distinct from the group. In boyhood he attained some degree of power and of mastery over the routine of living. Now he seems to proceed to the discovery of himself. This takes the form first of a desire for association with larger numbers of his contemporaries. Groups of playmates become bigger. There is a preference for games with definite rules involving the exact conformity of individuals to a prescribed procedure. The expectations of society (accompanied by differences in average rate of growth and changes in bodily structure) lead to greater differentiation between girls and boys. The girl discovers that she is a " girl ". The boy realises more clearly that he is a " boy ". The first consequence of this is a division into separate gangs or groups with distinct types of jokes and private topics of interest. (In co-educational schools this separation makes class-handling easier. The jokes of the girls neutralise those of the boys and there is less organised teasing of partially successful teachers.) The second consequence is a narrowing of the love-interest to one special friend of the same sex. Intimate secrets are shared with this friend—their nature varies with the past history of the individual and the traditions of the group.

This apparent narrowing of the love-interest continues in one form or another through the remainder of the adolescent period; and it persists into the early years of adult life. Its occurrence does not mean that all earlier bonds of affection are broken. For the fortunate adolescent the love of Mother and Father persists and develops in meaning and content. The admiration of teachers and other adults continues; and affectionate friendship with a variety of contemporaries survives. But over against these there is a new experience—more directly a forerunner of adult sex-relationships and mating. This has had precursors in fleeting forms at earlier stages—in special attachments to certain individuals.* Now it becomes more clearly particularised and more consciously related to the awareness of the self and the need for personal acceptance as an individual who is chosen and preferred before all others. At this stage it becomes especially important that the range of choice be not too narrow. If adolescents are segregated in single-sex schools (or even in single-sex clubs) there is a danger of a continuance of abnormal concentration

* The nature and extent of these vary very much with the expectations of the group, the character of the conversation overheard, and the behaviour observed by the growing child.

of affection on one person—a contemporary or a senior of the same sex—and false fears and distorted conceptions may be built up as to the characteristics of all persons of the opposite sex.

Co-education in a day-school is therefore particularly necessary for healthy emotional development; and it is through contact with their own parents in a home which is in wholesome relationship with a normal human community that a boy or girl can best be guided to social maturity.[8]

The next stage for many individuals is a conscious sensitivity to and admiration of an older person—usually a stranger—of the opposite sex. This is fostered by the expectations of the group, and varies in type with the degree of romantic anticipation and day-dreaming encouraged. Along with it the earlier loves continue. It is followed by a period of exploratory friendlinesses and temporary attachments (boy-friends, girl-friends, flirtations); and terminates in deliberate intention for most young adults by the definite selection of a mate. This is the ultimate socially acceptable narrowing of the love-interest; and it leads to the building of a home or "nest" into which are poured all the concentrated hopes and wishes of two young people who have finally graduated from adolescence to adult status.

The age at which such graduation is possible varies in differing social circles; but almost invariably it occurs nowadays many years after physical maturing; and in that fact many of the problems of the leader of adolescents find their explanation.

Little has been said of the physical and intellectual growth of the adolescent.[9] These aspects of development are more generally recognised than the special characteristics of his social and emotional maturing. All four aspects require to be understood by the teacher who is to sympathise with the nature and the needs of his pupils—at whichever stage they may be—sufficiently to enable him to take his place as their leader.

REFERENCES

1. cf. SUTTIE, I. D., *The Origins of Love and Hate*. Kegan Paul, 1935. An admirable exposition of the need for tenderness is given by G. E. CHESTERS in *The Mothering of Young Children*. Faber & Faber, 1943. See also

MURPHY, L. B., *Social Behavior and Child Personality*. Columbia Univ. Press, 1937; and

VALENTINE, C. W., *The Psychology of Early Childhood*. Methuen, 1942.

JERSILD, A. T., *Child Psychology*. Staples Press, Third Edition, 1947.

2. cf. MCCARTHY, D., *Language Development* in CARMICHAEL, L., *et al.*, *Manual of Child Psychology*. John Wiley, 1946 and 1954.

LEWIS, M. M., *Infant Speech.* Kegan Paul, 1936.

FLEMING, C. M., *Research and the Basic Curriculum.* Univ. of London Press, 1946 and 1952.

3. An interesting study of the social behaviour of a group of children is given in—

DIXON, C. M., *High, Wide and Deep.* Allen & Unwin, 1939.

4. cf. CABOT, E. L., *Seven Ages of Childhood.* Kegan Paul, 1921.

SAYLES, M. B., and NUDD, H. W., *The Problem Child in School.* Commonwealth Fund, 1925.

SAYLES, M. B., *The Problem Child at Home.* Commonwealth Fund, 1928.

SYMONDS, P. M., *The Psychology of Parent-Child Relationships.* D. Appleton Century, 1939.

MOODIE, W., *The Doctor and the Difficult Child.* Commonwealth Fund, 1940.

LEVY, D. M., *Maternal Overprotection.* Columbia Univ. Press, 1943.

YUDKIN, S., *All our Children.* Max Reinhardt, 1956.

HERBERT, W. L., and JARVIS, F. V., *Dealing with Delinquents.* Methuen, 1961.

5. STRANG, R., *et al.*, *Juvenile Delinquency and the Schools.* Forty-seventh Yearbook of the National Society for the Study of Education, Part 1, 1948.

6. ANASTASI, A., *et al.*, *Differential Psychology.* Macmillan, 1937 and 1949.

DEARBORN, W. F., *et al.*, *Predicting the Child's Development.* Sci. Art Publishers, 1941.

7. For useful discussions on recent findings see—

TAYLOR, K. W., *Do Adolescents need Parents?* D. Appleton-Century, 1938.

HURLOCK, E. B., *Adolescent Development.* McGraw-Hill, Second Edition, 1955.

MEAD, M., *et al.*, *Childhood in Contemporary Cultures.* Univ. of Chicago Press, 1955.

8. JONES, H. E., *Development in Adolescence.* D. Appleton-Century, 1943.

JERSILD, A. T., *The Psychology of Adolescence.* Macmillan, 1957.

STRANG, R., *The Adolescent Views Himself: A Psychology of Adolescence.* MacGraw-Hill, 1957.

WATTENBERG, W. W., *The Adolescent Years.* Harcourt Brace, 1957.

TAYLOR, K. W., *loc. cit.*

ZACHRY, C. B., *Emotion and Conduct in Adolescence.* D. Appleton Century, 1940.

9. FLEMING, C. M., *Adolescence: Its Social Psychology.* Routledge & Kegan Paul, 1948, 1955 and 1963.

CHAPTER XIII

MATURITY

TEACHERS can be leaders of young people because they are also persons; and the quality of their leadership depends not only on their understanding of their pupils but also on the degree to which they themselves succeed in being persons—sufficiently mature to take a place as adults in the adult community.

What are the characteristics of maturity? A partial answer to this has been given in previous chapters. Physical and intellectual maturing varies with glandular functioning; and individual differences range from what is called infantilism or idiocy to what may be described as marked superiority or genius. Emotional and social maturity are not dissociated from these; and in these also the differences between individuals are very great. Immaturity may be thought of as a perpetuation into adult life of modes of behaviour characteristic of infancy, childhood or adolescence, but imperfectly suited to the claims made by society upon the fully-grown human being. The problem of the parent or teacher is to foster growth by wise stimulation and adequate sustenance of body and spirit. The task of the learner is to use the opportunities provided and (through some realisation of the ideal at which he aims) to assist in the processes of his own education. Encouragement to growth is implicit in social life, in literature and in art; and capacity for growth is the counterpart of the individual's need for fresh experiences and fresh conquests.

Emotional maturing[1] results in changes both in the circumstances stimulating emotion and in the character of the individual's response. The fears of the infant appear to be associated with physical insecurities. He is small and weak. Sudden noises and the unexpected removal of support produce reactions of the nature of those which adults characterise in themselves as fear; and the responses are immediate, very complete and uncontrolled by thought or the consequences of experience. The fears of the child are a partial sequel to his awareness of his own very limited knowledge. They reflect the educational influences to which he has been subjected and they therefore vary widely from one group to another. Fears of the dark, of ghosts, of bogies, of fire, of pirates, of wild animals, have their basis in the immensity of the unknown world which surrounds the growing child; but they have their immediate antecedents in remarks made by the adults in his circle. (These may have been intended as a reassurance against the occurrence of an expected fear.) The fortunate child escapes most of these terrors, and is progressively comforted by the stability of the protecting love of parents and friends.

The fears of the adolescent are of the type of social distresses. He has learnt that not all loud noises denote danger, and that there are no tigers behind the couch; but he is still unsure of himself as a member of society. He is afraid of being snubbed. He fears that he may do the wrong thing. He is still self-centred and "shy". The responses he makes are not so immediate nor so complete. (He does not cry out or run away, and concomitant physical changes are less obvious.) And to a varying degree, dependent on the traditions of his group, he has discovered the satisfactions which result from such postponement and control. His self-respect is increased to the degree to which he deliberately conquers fear. By the time adult status is reached, most of the fears of childhood and adolescence have become unreal. The socially-experienced adult has discovered the techniques of entrance to a party. He no longer believes that everyone is critical of him or watching him. He knows what lies behind the closed doors of workshop, office, bank, hotel, or public-house; and he knows how his group expects him to behave in each. He is less physically weak, less ignorant, and less socially insecure. For him there remain the "reasonable" fears of ill-health, unemployment, the perils of traffic, the possibilities of accident, and other distresses associated with his knowledge of communal responsibilities and world politics. Emotional maturing in relation to fear does not mean that fear has ceased to exist; but it implies a progressive elimination of unreasoning fear and a progressive decrease in associated terrors. At any time, however, there may be a regression—traceable perhaps to exhaustion, hunger, illness or anxiety. The adult may behave in a fashion more suited to infancy, childhood or adolescence. And there are many adults who seem rarely to succeed in maintaining continuous behaviour at anything approximating to the adult level. The conception of age-performance has become familiar in relation to the discussion of what is commonly called intelligence. Something comparable to mental age is observable also in a study of what may be described as emotional maturing.

Similar stages may be noted in the conditions provoking anger, in the reactions produced by it, and in the observable regressions to behaviour representative of earlier levels. The infant is provoked to displays of "anger" over physical thwartings and restraints. The school child is less affected by mere contact; but he resents removal of playthings and interruptions of activity. The adolescent shows passion over social slights affecting himself; and the adult is made indignant by injustices affecting his family, his professional group, his city or his state.

The emotion of love likewise shows progressive changes from the tenderness of infancy through the affection of childhood and the widening friendlinesses of adolescence to the concentrated passion of sexual love and its canalising of affection into narrower channels. After this concentration (whose characteristic outward expression is the establishment of a home and devotion to children) there comes, to those adults who continue to mature, a later extension of the love-interest. This takes the form of widening social contacts beyond the limits of the household; and shows itself as concern for the welfare of the district, the community, the nation or the world. It is no accident that the happily married, after absorbed attention to the needs of their own children in their twenties (or early thirties), turn again to outside interests such as politics, club-membership, or religious organisations in the late thirties or forties. Fortunate are the children whose parents continue to develop into such adult preoccupations; and fortunate are the pupils whose teachers have passed through comparable stages. Not all human beings have children of their own. Not all human beings engage in sexual intercourse; but all may make the transition from the narrowness of a love-interest centred on their own most intimate circle to a concern with the world outside. To the degree to which they do this they may be said to have become emotionally mature.

A similar sort of progression may be traced in the nature and the range of other interests. For fortunate children there is a comparable extension in the choice of activities through the years of school life, and a later limitation of these in concentration upon a "job" and its responsibilities (or a profession and its demands) in the years immediately afterwards.

For those who continue to mature, this narrowing is followed by a widening of outlook in which the profession or job falls into place as one of the many very interesting things that require to be done.

Not all adults mature to this level. The teacher, for example, may be said to be arrested at the late adolescent stage, who, at the age of, say, thirty-five, is not a householder taking a share in the life of the community—with interests and activities beyond the limits of her profession. The same is true of the shop-assistant or the business man whose interests are so limited or so feeble that "leisure" time has to be "killed" and boredom is an actuality.

"The world is so full of a number of things." The world

is full of potential friends, entertaining possibilities, and undertakings of genuine importance.

The personal maturity of adult mental health follows upon this recognition and is accompanied by an experience of inner confidence and security symbolised by a self-forgetfulness which permits either joy or sorrow to be met without undue distress. Such adult independence is rooted in the fuller understanding which comes from a philosophy of life or awareness of religious experience ; and it also is found in differing degrees comparable to the differences in the development of independence observable in the physical progression from infancy to adult status.

Some understanding of the manifestations of maturity is useful to a teacher not merely as an aid to the assessment of his own actions but as a guide to the type of development to be expected from his pupils and as a clue to the factors conditioning their behaviour.

Many of the responses of children are irritating to adults when viewed as things-in-themselves and distressing when considered as manifestations of instinctive tendencies or primitive urges. When judged in the light of their origins in the reactions of immature organisms under social pressures of varying kinds, they become both more comprehensible and less formidable ; and the observable changes in their forms justify a belief in the possibility of educational modifications of human behaviour. The greater the sympathy and the personal maturity of the teacher the more completely will he be fortified against unnecessary disappointment. The wider his interests and the more balanced his own development the easier does such fortitude become. His progress towards full status as a person while including physical and intellectual maturing, passes on to a generalised love-interest and a freedom from anger and fear which render personal regression less frequent and permit fuller understanding and wiser treatment of the regressions of other human beings—as individuals or in groups.

REFERENCES

1. cf. Hollingworth, L. S., *The Adolescent Child*, in Murchison, C., (ed.) *A Handbook of Child Psychology*. Clark Univ. Press, 1933.
Arlitt, A. H., *Adolescent Psychology*. Allen & Unwin, 1937.

PART IV

LEARNING IS SOMETIMES MISDIRECTED

CHAPTER XIV

EDUCATIONAL FAILURES

" IT is never too late to learn." This sentence echoes mockingly in the ears of educators who have tried to produce changes in human behaviour and appear to have failed—the parents of the girl who is " out of control ", the teachers of the boy who is " no good at figures ", the foremen of the worker who has " no ability to concentrate ", the club-leaders of the young people who are " lacking in a sense of purpose ", the probation officer or magistrates who deal with habitual offenders who have been " well warned ". It seems desirable at this point to give brief consideration to the difficulties typified by such examples of what seem to be educational failures.

Jean was " out of parental control ". She was reported to the police for refusing to return home at a reasonable hour and for open defiance of parental demands. Enquiry showed that she was an adopted child—taken at the age of four, petted and dressed as a beautiful doll until about the age of seven and then rejected. Her foster-parents had a son of their own about the same age. Her earliest recollections were of this boy being taken to the Pictures and her being left, of the boy being allowed to bring home his friends and her being forbidden to bring hers, of his receiving presents and her being forgotten. Her " mother " showed her no affection. Her " father " paid her no attention. She had no recollection of having been taken for walks or played with by either parent since about the age of seven. Her home was a home in which nothing interesting or entertaining ever happened. It was not her club ; her family was not her gang.

She left school at fourteen, went to work, and there made friends with an older girl who had a " boy-friend who had a friend ". The four of them—two boys and two girls—went together to the Park or the Pictures. There was nowhere else to go. Nothing very exciting happened there ; but her " mother " tried to deprive her of this, her only pleasure, and she rebelled. The form her rebellion took was socially unwise ; but it was for the most part a consequence of the educational influences to which she had been submitted, and it represented a conformity to the standards of the only group which had genuinely given her acceptance and recognition.

Sandy was one of the many boys and girls who enter the Infant School with considerable knowledge of arithmetical concepts and a fair skill in the manipulation of numbers. His mother had been a teacher of Mathematics; and he had been wisely handled and encouraged to believe in his own adequacy in the ordinary situations and adventures of home life. There was every reason to anticipate a successful school career, and every probability that Arithmetic and Mathematics would hold no terror. To the surprise of the parents he early showed distaste for school; and when term reports—those psychologically unsound instruments for child torture—began to appear they recorded that he was "very poor at number", had "no head for figures" and was "lacking in co-operativeness and energy". Patient questioning and enquiry by the parents ultimately revealed something of what had been done to him by stupid handling in the formative first months at school. He had, on his arrival, been profoundly shocked by being labelled as a "baby" and put into the "baby-class"—he who was the oldest son in the household and a friend of his mother and father. He had, at home, been accustomed to be treated as a reasonable human being. He was now given three beans to look at and was allowed to move them only according to instructions. School soon became a place where one was bored and in which one found relief either by day-dreaming or by clandestine activities. At a later stage, when the Arithmetic became more worthy of his attention, his reviving interest was damped by a blue pencil which every day marked as "wrong" his most careful efforts. He discovered after many weeks that what was "wrong" was that each exercise should have begun at a specified point on the page; but by that time he had given up wishing to achieve success through arithmetical prowess and had been accepted by the group among whom it was "good form" to do badly in class. Teacher and school were both rejected in his thinking; and it was not until many years later—in his middle adolescence—that an understanding teacher succeeded in reversing this attitude and reviving in school affairs the energy and co-operativeness which he had continued to display in his home life.

Tim's school reports persistently recorded that he was "lacking in concentration", "easily distracted", and "could do better if he tried harder". His father was disappointed and scolded him once every term when the report arrived. His mother at more frequent intervals told him how little she thought of him. When he went to work his foreman made the same sort of remark.

His father was a chemist who had attained considerable success in research work. He had no other hobby, no outside interests and a very limited circle of friends. His ideal of home was of a neat place—pleasantly furnished and peaceful. Tim as a baby had proved an undesirable interruption to his father's sleep and a source of noise and dirt. Both noise and dirt were therefore suppressed as far as possible. Tim was forbidden to make loud sounds. He was prevented from playing with earth or water. He was continually interrupted whenever he embarked on any fascinating enterprise of his own. (He was being " naughty " or " dirty " or not " doing what he was told " or " getting in father's way ".) As a consequence he grew up without experience of the satisfactions resulting from concentration and with none of that interest in present activities which later forms an important ingredient in mental health.

At school, unfortunately, little was done to modify this personality pattern. The teachers were not so unwise as the parents had been ; but instruction was too completely on class lines and he did not experience the satisfying absorption which results from the skilful use of self-instructive material in Arithmetic and silent-study readers in English. As a result he still remained markedly unable to concentrate. Correction of the defect would have been more difficult at the school stage. It became still harder to overcome when adult status was reached.[1]

That re-education would not have been impossible is, however, evidenced by the increase in concentrative endeavour often secured by occupational therapists who attempt re-habilitation in the light of the principles of educational psychology. Patients incapacitated by injury and rendered depressed and indifferent in outlook as a result of long illness can (through the skilful use of suggestion—appealing to their fundamental needs for acceptance, fresh experience, and the exercise of responsibility) be led to a willingness to attempt new tasks. They can be trained until they are able to secure self-forgetfulness in absorbed concentration on the reaching of an attainable objective.

Through a variety of circumstances this was not attempted in Tim's case. He left the district and nothing is known of his later development.

Dick was a thief. He was also a liar. All sorts of evidence accumulated against him. The tale need hardly be recounted ; but the culminating point was reached when he took money from his brother's money-box and tried to run away to London. When charged with theft he " told another lie ". (That was no more than his parents expected since for many years they had " believed nothing that he ever said " and " trusted him only as far as they saw him ".)

Dick, when examined, proved to be a dull child with an eye

defect and a somewhat underdeveloped body. He had been a rejected baby. Both his mother and father were, in his early infancy, too busy with other things to be bothered with him. At a later stage a younger brother had proved both brighter and more acceptable. Dick was short-sighted and, therefore, appeared timid. His father was ashamed of him and told him so. His I.Q. was about 80; and every term the school report repeated that he was poor at Arithmetic and backward in Reading. No one stopped to enquire the reason. Both school and home failed in this respect. He stayed away from school. He turned sick with anxiety. He told more lies to cover the consequences. The money from the money-box was admittedly taken to buy a railway ticket because he had decided that the best thing he could do for his mother was to disappear so that she would never be troubled with him again. He had accepted only too completely the family group's apparent estimation of himself; and had gauged only too accurately their scarcely veiled wish to be rid of him. His father was a commercial traveller who, in his gayer moments, told stories of the ways in which he tricked his customers. Both mother and father told "white" lies freely to the neighbours in connection with various episodes in family life. Neither parent realised that their educative influences had been all in the direction of lying and stealing; and that the whole picture of life which they had built up for Dick through the years merely met its completion in the theft and the truancy (which they resented chiefly because of the social stigma attached to overt disgrace).

Molly was a maladjusted girl. At the age of sixteen she ran away with a boy of twenty-two and lived with him for three months in another city before the police found her and returned her unprotesting to her home. She was thoroughly dejected and defeated. "All my bright ideas turn out to be no good." This one had been no exception to the rule.

Enquiry showed an instability of temperament which had a long educational history behind it. Nervous anxieties had showed themselves early. She was "different from other girls". She could not travel in a bus or car without turning sick. Her father had died when she was eight, and her mother had gone out to work. She had come home each afternoon to an empty house and had had to get a meal for herself and a younger sister. She had no friends in the village. She had won a scholarship to a Secondary School and was, therefore, in that respect also "different from the others". At the Secondary School she was again an isolate. The other girls all travelled in buses and she went by train. The teachers did not like her. She did not like any of them. Into this setting came Albert. He liked her. He told her she was " wonderful " and she, believing that everything would be " marvellous ", followed him out of school and away from home.

This was her version of her life-story. By themselves none of these handicaps need have led her into delinquencies. Very many children have home circumstances as difficult as these. In her case, however, there seems to have been no steadying or counter-balancing influence. Her mother was herself intensely self-centred and unhappy. She was almost completely lacking in protecting love ; and, while she had provided food and clothes, she had satisfied scarcely any of the other needs of her child. When Molly was in difficulty her mother always took the side of the accuser. The smallest misdemeanours were reported to neighbours and friends. Molly stole a chocolate. Molly told a lie. " Molly is a most disappointing child." " You can put no trust in Molly." And Molly conformed only too well to the pattern suggested to her. She became a " difficult child " and progressed through small lies and petty thefts to the culminating episode which brought her to the attention of the police.

REFERENCE

1. For an interesting discussion of results of testing such unstable children see ABRAMSON, J., *L'Enfant et l'Adolescent Instables.* Presses Universitaires de France, 1940.

CHAPTER XV

TREATMENT

WHAT can be done to help children who are in such difficulties? The initial step in every instance is to try to understand the child—his needs, his interests, his abilities, his wishes and the degree to which the formative influences in his life have been directed towards the frustration or the satisfaction of his requirements. The immediate advantage of such an attempt at understanding is that it may reveal to the child for the first time that someone is genuinely interested in him and concerned about his welfare. It is also likely to result in greater sympathy on the part of the adult. Its danger is that it may over-emphasise a passing misdemeanour and concentrate attention on a bad habit which will more easily be dropped if it is forgotten.

In the school situation the position is relatively simple. Teachers have the means available to enable them to make skilful assessment of the present performance of a pupil in tests of achievement, or in tests of intelligence in its various forms. They have access to assistance in the interpretation of the statistics obtainable from the use of group tests.* They can judge the degree to which a pupil is retarded or advanced; and something is known of methods by which instruction can be adapted to individual differences.† Teachers have also some knowledge of the processes involved in learning; and they are aware of the importance of arranging for a class-room situation in which the social relationships are such that the pupil believes he can learn, wishes to learn and is prepared to take the necessary steps to achieve learning. This does not mean that teaching is easy; but guidance within the school situation is so much supported by the prestige of the school and the traditions behind the educational system, that for the majority of children no other specific agencies are required. Most juvenile delinquents grow up into self-respecting citizens.[1] Most self-respecting citizens have had to be sharply taught, at one time or other, that certain experimental behaviour of theirs was described by their circle as "telling lies", "stealing", "bullying", "misbehaving"; and they have decided to discontinue such actions in order to win the acceptance of the group to which they belong.

Unsatisfactory scholastic achievement repays study from many points of view. When, for example, the reading age or arith-

* cf. references given above in Chapters I and II.
† cf. references in Chapters VII and XI.

metic age (or the standardised score in any school subject) is definitely lower than the mental age (or standardised score in a group test of general mental ability), it is desirable to make as full enquiries as possible as to the attitude of the home and the past history of the pupil.

For this reason, time spent on personal contact with parents is usually more profitably employed than a corresponding number of hours spent in transcribing term reports. Since the aim of schooling is to modify behaviour, the energies of teachers are more usefully expended in studying children in relation to the formative influences of their family and their community than in classifying or labelling their isolated attributes. (Written recording also often serves to perpetuate passing weaknesses by giving official status to a description which, in many cases, might have been only temporarily true.) " Careless ", " Untidy ", " Lacking in self-confidence ", " Poor at reading ", " Somewhat unsociable ", " Inarticulate ", " Shows little promise ", " Poor linguistic ability ", " No ear for music ". Remarks like these have been observed to depress rather than to stimulate ; and pupils have been noticed to come to believe in their own inadequacy to a degree which prevents a genuine effort after improvement. (The therapeutic value of mere scolding is much less than seems commonly believed.) And, on the other hand, over-emphasis on what the teacher may have to report at the end of every ten or twelve weeks tends to foster a habit of working for the sake of a reward (or for fear of punishment) rather than a delight in present activities and an interest in the fresh experiences involved in the routine learning-programme of a good school.

Failures in learning may be traceable to lowness of intelligence, physical defects (in eyesight, hearing, or glandular development), unsuitable feeding, inadequate sleep, lack of equipment, or unwise methods of tuition.[2] All of these deserve careful consideration ; but along with all these go the consequences of certain experiences which may be called social—the treatment the pupil has received in the presence of his group and his reaction to that treatment, the suggestions that have been made to him and his response to those suggestions, the patterns of behaviour that he has had the chance of observing and the means he has adopted in his attempt to imitate what he has admired.

For a minority of pupils more specialised treatment than the school can give may prove necessary. They may require to be " taught " through the additional prestige attached to Clinics or to Juvenile Courts. The parent or the teacher may appeal to the authority of the Magistrate, the Probation Officer or the Psychologist.

It is important, however, to realise that for most of these

difficult cases the treatment needed is again educational in character. In many instances educational influences have to be deliberately directed to the parents or guardians. The re-education of parents is a harder task than the education of a child; but it is achieved by quite similar means. There is evidence, for example, that direct instructions or weighty warnings (whether by Magistrates or Psychologists) produce defiance or result in indifference. Advice has to rise to the level of suggestion before it will be accepted; and evidence is accumulating that the most useful team for the purpose consists of educational psychologist and visiting teacher—both skilled in the psychology of learning, experienced as social workers, and with the prestige of the whole educational service behind them. Such a team can make a very thorough study of present conditions and formative influences. They can give guidance as to reasonable hours of sleep and of exercise. They can encourage an adequate variety of diet; and they can foster a change of attitude on the part of the home or the school. Through personal tuition of the child they can also, in most instances, revive hope and reawaken confidence; and they can utilise the therapeutic contributions which can be made by available community agencies.

For a small minority of remaining recalcitrant cases reference from the Educational Clinic to specialised medical treatment may be found desirable. A small proportion of children suffer from disorders suitable for treatment by a psycho-pathologist; and a small number require the prescription of special vitamin preparations or glandular extracts. For these there is reason to believe that the best provision will, probably, in the future, be made by their reference to a local Municipal or County hospital where a team of physicians (with adequate laboratory assistance) can co-operate in their treatment. Child Guidance Clinics have in the past done admirable exploratory work in the psychiatric treatment of difficult children; but developments in medical science (both in endocrinology and in the treatment of mental disorders by shock therapy, by insulin, and by vitamin preparations), have revealed the limitations of treatment open to a team consisting merely of a psycho-analyst and a psychiatric social worker.[3]

What can a teacher do with regard to personality disorders for which there are as yet no standardised tests and which do not appear to emerge as a direct consequence of a school situation? What can a club-leader do for a girl like Molly or a boy like Dick?

Here again direct lecturing or scolding is of little avail. Education is not a matter of mere instruction. Certain observations can, however, be made. Re-direction of energy and revival of hope can be attempted. Increase of self-respect through the discovery of some activity in which success can be attained is often the most urgent need of such boys and girls. The club-leader who complains that all young people are "lacking in a sense of purpose" is chiefly revealing his own imperfect knowledge of youth and his lack of success in appealing to their interests. (The form which these interests will take will, of course, vary from district to district, and from season to season—with changes in type of work, degree of exhaustion, absence of opportunities for initiative, etc., etc.) The headmaster who expels a boy who is "not a credit to the school" merely advertises the fact that his school has failed in skill and patience.

The school or the club has as its first problem the establishment of social relationships in which its suggestions have a chance of being accepted. It can then as a general precaution let it be known that it, as a group, stands for certain points of view. Such definite guidance is now believed to be a more sound procedure (both on educational and on psychological grounds) than the adoption of the *laissez-faire* attitude which was formerly advocated as a result of over-emphasis on the universality, fixity, and strength of certain so-called instincts. Adolescents need acceptance by an admired group. They are seeking for such approval even through behaviour which seems most reprehensible; and much greater ultimate maladjustment results from the absence of suitable direction than from a leadership informed by wisdom and loving-kindness. "It is better to do this." "These are our reasons for doing this." "You can help us if you do this." "We do not do that." "But we like you. You may always count on our friendship." "Make a fresh start." "We need your help and we bear no grudges because of past mistakes." (After condemnation or reproof it is important to reaffirm the reality of the affection—or love—which the offender still enjoys. "Nothing that you do can alter the fact that we love you; but we object to that behaviour. We cannot approve of that." Threats, for example, that "Mother will not love you any more" are both untrue to human experience and destructive of the security necessary for wholesome development. On both grounds they are to be avoided.)

Sex problems of adolescence cannot be evaded by mere lectures on biological facts. Such information is necessary and can quite simply be made available [4]; but, in addition, the boy or girl needs initiation into the traditions and the experience of the group. Clinical records make it clear that abstention in itself is not harmful and that marital adjustment and the rearing of happy and healthy children are rendered more difficult by sex experiences before or outside marriage.[5] The issue involves a choice between a passing impulse and a more mature personal and social experience. Successful marriage is worth striving for. "That other game is not worth the candle." This need not always be said to all adolescents in direct terms. Celebrations of happy marriages and scarcely audible remarks to the effect that an admired baby was "worth waiting for" may be all that is necessary. Support for clean living—directly or indirectly—is widespread in literature and art, and much psychological insight is obtainable through the impersonal discussion of books, films and broadcasts.

Such class-room or club discussion may be compared with the developing technique of group-analysis mentioned in Chapter III.[6] The healing value of talk about problems of intense human interest is beginning to be rediscovered by educational psychologists. (It has long been recognised by religious bodies which lay emphasis on the intellectual content of church services.) Personal questions can often find an answer through corporate consideration of topics which are not admitted to be particularly relevant to any one member of the group; and relief can come both through the application of general principles to specific experiences and through the lessening of a sense of isolation consequent on a realisation of kinship in the face of problems common to all.

A simple opportunity of starting such discussions may occur through comments made by club-members on the content of the many admirable novels, stories, biographies or poems which contain material relevant to contemporary life. The reading of such books provides opportunities for the enlargement of adolescent experience. It offers adventures in living and a means by which the world can be explored. Impersonal discussion of consequent discoveries (when invited by the adolescent) may give a club-leader or teacher the chance of contributing to the personal maturing of the young person in his charge. He is, however, a wise guide who does not admit that he has noticed that he is leading the way. (Rarely need he hope to have the satisfaction of being quite sure that he has done so.)

A similar stance may require to be taken with regard to other social issues; and similar means of dealing with them are available. Addiction to strong drink often begins in a craving for popularity—a wish to be accepted as one of a group. It may continue as a device for the relief of boredom or anxiety. Protection against it is best achieved not through mere information as to the damaging effect of alcohol, but through the substitution of more mature means of attaining social standing and a sense of mental well-being.[7] "Somewhat immature." "A childish way of behaving." "I am disappointed that she is not more grown up." Indirect remarks may again be more effective than direct commands.

Under fortunate circumstances very many such problems of course do not arise. As has been indicated above in Chapter XII, many so-called sex problems do not arise in co-educational day-schools or genuinely co-educational clubs. They are not a necessary part of human development nor an evidence of the primacy of the sexual instinct. They are culturally as well as hereditarily conditioned; and their incidence varies widely both from individual to individual and from group to group.

Children brought up in institutions suffer certain emotional and social deprivations from which later recovery is difficult. They tend to be too dependent on the traditions of the group, and they miss the nightly reassurance of a family-life in which they regain individual status and receive a high degree of recognition and personal acceptance. They are also, as a rule, exposed to contact with too limited a group of adults and too homogeneous a circle of children. It is probably on this account that they seem especially liable to emotional upsets and somewhat abnormally sensitive to sexual stimuli when they emerge from the artificial segregation of a residential school into ordinary life outside.

Experimental evidence on the incidence of behaviour disorders or educational failures in private boarding schools as compared with day-schools is difficult to obtain, but comparable studies of State orphanages as contrasted with foster homes appear to favour the latter—on emotional and social as well as on intellectual grounds.

Arguments in favour of single-sex schools on the ground of differences in the interests and the rate of development of boys and girls are based on a misinterpretation which over-emphasises the importance of an average score, and fails to note the implications of the wide degree of overlap at each age.[8] The differences in average score between boys and girls on most measurable attributes are now known to be so small as to be barely significant; and the differences within each sex group at any age are much greater than the differences between group averages. Boys and girls are also persons. Their abilities and interests vary according to their personal endowment and the treatment they have received. Prediction of suitable training is not possible on the score of sex alone.

It is also beginning to be doubted whether the dichotomy of masculine-feminine is any more useful as a means of describing human beings than the comparable contrasts of submissive-aggressive, extravert-introvert, follower-leader. It is possible to define what is meant by each term; but human beings have a way of slipping from one category to another at different stages of growth and under differing educational influences. Some men are on some occasions more feminine than many women. Some women are more masculine than many men. Once again it is desirable to observe human beings as they show themselves to be in the shifting social relationships of the family or the group; and, in this connection also, the more mature individual has the more balanced personality with greater flexibility of adjustment and greater width of interests—able to be submissive or aggressive, co-operative or resistant, a spectator or a performer, according to the requirements of the situation. The less well-balanced individual who shows rigidity of response—who is unable ever to allow his friends to be themselves but must always have them either as followers or as leaders—may be said to be suffering from a learning-experience which has been misdirected. He also is in need of re-education. And, lest it be thought that it is only parents, teachers, pupils or club leaders who are to be subjected to educational influences, it may be remarked again that the processes involved in the re-education of Magistrates, Members of Parliament, Employers of Labour and the like are entirely similar to those employable under school conditions.

All human beings are also persons. All resent somewhat the approach of the law-giver: "Thou shalt not" . . . All may be reached by the wise teacher who commends rather than instructs: "Blessed are they who" . . . The good teacher is something of a public speaker. He can win attention. But he is more of a psycho-therapist. He uses suggestion. He believes that education is possible; and he can (if he is skilful enough) transform Simon the unstable into Peter the rock-like.

REFERENCES

1. cf. GLUECK, S., and GLUECK, E. T., *Juvenile Delinquents Grown Up*. Commonwealth Fund, 1942.
2. cf. BRUECKNER, L. J., *et al.*, *Educational Diagnosis*. Thirty-fourth Yearbook of the National Society for the Study of Education. Public School Publishing Company, 1935.
   BURT, C., *The Backward Child*. Univ. of London Press, 1937.
   SCHONELL, F. J., *Backwardness in the Basic Subjects*. Oliver & Boyd, 1942.
3. PLANT, J. S., *Personality and the Cultural Pattern*. The Commonwealth Fund, 1937.
   cf. MURRAY, H. A., *Explorations in Personality*. Oxford Univ. Press, 1938; and
   ROGERS, C. R., *The Clinical Treatment of the Problem Child*. Houghton Mifflin, 1939.
   See also: STERN, H. H., *Child Neglect and the Teaching and Learning of the Maternal Role*, "Case Conference", 2, 2, 4–14, 1955.
   STERN, H. H., *Parent Education and Parental Learning*. Ph.D. Thesis University of London, 1956.

GARSIDE, A., *A Study of the Wishes as to their Children's Development Expressed by a Group of Parents of Primary School Children.* M.A. Thesis, London, 1956.

4. For useful statements see—
KELIHER, A. V., *Life and Growth.* D. Appleton Century, 1938.
HACKER, R., *Telling the Teen-Ager.* Deutsch, 1957.

5. TAYLOR, K. W., *Do Adolescents need Parents?* D. Appleton Century, 1938.
MACE, D. R., *Does Sex Morality Matter?* Rich and Cowan, 1943.
See also representative references and extracts in—
STERN, B. J., *The Family Past and Present.* D. Appleton Century, 1938, especially p. 412 f.

6. An accessible description along with a good bibliography is given in—
BIERER, J., *Group Psychotherapy,* "British Medical Journal", Feb. 14th, 1942.
See also:
MORENO, H. L., (ed.), *Group Psychotherapy: A Symposium.* Beacon House, 1945.

7. cf. MEYER, F. M., *The Psychology and Treatment of Alcohol Addicts,* "British Journal of Medical Psychology", 4, 1943, pp. 381–7.
MORENO, J. L., *loc. cit.*
With this may be compared: MORENO, J. L., *Who Shall Survive?* Beacon House, 1953.
MORENO, J. L., *Sociometry and the Science of Man.* Beacon House, 1956.

8. For summaries of evidence on sex differences see—
FREEMAN, F. S., *Individual Differences.* Harrap, 1934.
BURT, C. *How the Mind Works.* Allen & Unwin, 1935.
FLEMING, C. M., *Adolescence: Its Social Psychology.* Routledge & Kegan Paul, 1948, 1955 and 1963.

CHAPTER XVI

CONCLUSIONS: A BRIEF SUMMARY

1. THE construction of standardised tests for the assessment of personal characteristics and the measurement of human abilities has made it possible to study the behaviour of individuals and of groups with greatly increased accuracy. Through the use of such instruments a teacher can learn in a few hours as much about the present performance of his pupils as he could formerly have discovered in many months of ordinary class-room or club contacts. It is, therefore, desirable for educators to become familiar with the administration of such tests and with the interpretation of statistical terms often used in discussion of their results.

2. Standardised tests also permit comparisons between one class and another; and the objectivity of their scoring makes them largely independent of the personal prejudices of an examiner.

3. A study of individuals at the beginning of the twentieth century led to interpretations of conduct which emphasised the strength of instinctive tendencies. These descriptions somewhat minimised the variability of human behaviour in differing circumstances, and tempted observers to expect greater consistency and a lesser degree of educability than seems justified by closer study of the changing social relationships of ordinary life.

4. The development of clinical psychology was followed by increased awareness of the implications of social maladjustment in problem children, in delinquents and in criminals. Attention began to be given to means by which the needs of human beings may meet satisfaction; and careful analyses were made of the social consequences of frustration.

5. Propagation of opinions is achieved through the offering of some satisfaction of these primary human needs (the wish for affection, for social acceptance, for membership of an admired group, for fresh adventures, new ideas and a consciousness of personal responsibility).

6. A study of needs implies some recognition of the significance of the interactions of an individual and his social background. It results in an attempt to understand not only his present state and the formative influences which have affected his development but also his future expectations, his attitudes, motives and wishes. All of these determine the methods and the processes by which education can be effected.

7. Changes in human behaviour may be initiated by individuals who act upon groups through suggestions made effective by the prestige associated with a type of leadership which appeals to the specific characteristics of the group.

8. They may be effected by groups who influence individuals through the social controls associated with the conditions attached to entry to membership. Requirements vary with the nature of the activities of the group and the characteristics of its members ; and the reaction of individuals may take the form of indifference, of refusal, or of a willingness to conform which is consequent upon a desire for acceptance by that particular group.

9. The characteristics and the wishes of a group may at any time be changed by the addition of a new member. They may also be modified through the loss of a member. Group activities show sensitivity to quite small changes in social atmosphere.

10. Learning takes place not as a consequence of mere subjection to impressions nor from mere repetition of experiences. It requires activity on the part of the learner ; and its most characteristic form is that of the "insight" which results from an understanding of the meaning of a new activity and a recognition of its place in a total pattern.

11. Changes in behaviour result either from changes in the total situation in which an individual finds himself or from alterations in its meaning to him. Habits can, therefore, be altered if their significance is modified. Actions willingly performed in one context may appear to be impossible in another.

12. Learning is also dependent on the level of maturation of the learner ; and it seems to take place by a series of successive clarifications of concepts, increments in skill, or modifications in attitude. It is consequent on willing continuance of practice accompanied by expectations of success.

13. Reinforcement of learning accompanies favourable attitudes towards the place, the instructor or the material of learning. It is also facilitated by knowledge of success and by the positive incentives of encouragement and praise. (The most effective class-room motivation follows from such awareness of progress accompanied by an understanding of the meaning of the activity in which the pupil is engaged. The least effective instruments which a teacher can use are sarcasm, ridicule, public reprimand, or punishment through extra work or low marks.)

14. Disappointment, defeat, and absence of hope are depressive agents. Persistence is closely related to experience of the satisfactions of concentrated endeavour in an atmosphere of social acceptance.

15. Learning is practically co-extensive with living and is not merely a characteristic of childhood and youth. Its cessation in

any field is a sequel to deliberate intention or to absence of the opportunities for growth. It may be resumed when a change in circumstances or a change in wishes results in a change in attitude.

16. Pupils belong to many groups. The most important of these is the home; and within a family intrinsic characteristics such as interests, ambitions, and attitudes exercise greater influence than extrinsic attributes such as size, mere completeness of structure, or economic circumstances. The good home is measurable in terms of personal relationships and human responses rather than in terms of parental status, tidiness or prosperity.

17. Community influences reach individuals through the mediation of smaller groups; and within one district or one country there are wide individual variations.

18. School influences facilitate learning through the social stimulation they can offer. Behaviour is modifiable within the limits set by an original endowment whose potentialties are as yet only imperfectly understood.

19. Attitudes of teachers and attitudes towards teachers have an important influence on observable behaviour; and responses vary in different sorts of social atmosphere. Behaviour is a function not merely of the character of an individual but of the treatment given to him both by the teacher and by other members of a group. Democratic treatment results in the highest type of class-room morale (with greater flexibility of response, greater independence of judgment and better social cohesion). This helps to account for the measured success of school methods which seek to adapt instruction to the needs, interests and abilities of pupils and to produce socialised behaviour by opportunities for co-operative endeavour.

20. It also serves to account partially for the observable fact that marked changes in performance are known to occur in the course of growth (especially during adolescence). Long-term studies of individuals are beginning to reveal the dangers of too early prediction and too rigid selection and classification. Human beings are essentially educable; and educational guidance to be effective must be continuous—if training is to be genuinely adapted to their characteristics and their needs.

21. Many of the responses of children are irritating when viewed as things in themselves and distressing when considered as manifestations of instinctive tendencies or primitive urges. When judged in the light of their origins in the reactions of immature organisms under social pressures of varying kinds, they become both more comprehensible and less formidable.

Most of the above findings have been expressed in terms of teacher and pupil. They are equally applicable (in slightly differing terminology) to the problems which arise in other educational situations—whether these involve foremen and workmen, employees and managers, husbands and wives, sisters and brothers or parents and children. Educating is not easy but it is possible. In all social settings educability—flexibility of response and adaptability—is an observable characteristic of human behaviour.

APPENDIX

EXERCISE I

WHICH THE READER IS INVITED TO TRY BEFORE READING CHAPTER ONE

1. You have met many new teachers. . . . When you read the words " new teacher ", of which new teacher do you think first ?

Write a description of that teacher, of the circumstances accompanying your meeting, and the impressions you formed.

2. Which of the following sorts of shop-window interests you most ?
   (*a*) a book shop,
   (*b*) an ironmonger's,
   (*c*) a grocer's,
   (*d*) a chemist's,
   (*e*) a milliner's,
   (*f*) a sports outfitter's,
   (*g*) a gown shop.
3. What do you believe to be your chief needs ?
4. In what ways have these needs been satisfied in your life so far ?

EXERCISE II

TO BE CARRIED OUT, IF POSSIBLE, BY A GROUP OF FRIENDS

1. On a piece of paper make rows of dots like this. . . . . as rapidly as you can for two minutes.

How many did you make ?

2. What thoughts came into your mind as you worked ?
3. Have you any comments to make on the method of working and the personal characteristics of the quickest member of the group ?
4. Think of a favourite shop-window seen recently and then, as fast as you can, for two minutes write the names of all the articles you last saw in it. When next you see it, compare your list with its contents. Have you a good memory ? (This may also be tried as a competition between friends describing the contents of one familiar shop-window.)

EXERCISE III

ASSOCIATED IDEAS

Here is an experiment to try with a friend.

1. How fast can you write words which come into your mind one after the other ? Take a piece of paper. (Ask your friend to help by noting the time.) Begin with the word " school " and write as quickly as you can—one below the other—all the words which come into your mind. Write them just as they come. Stop writing after exactly two minutes.
2. Ask your friend to do the same. Then look at your lists and

see if you can remember the thoughts or emotions associated with each word that you wrote. Do you know the reason for any of the associations ?

(The experiment you have just tried is sometimes described as a test of " free association ". Its results are important in the history of psycho-analysis.)

3. What do you wish for most ? Compare your answer with that of a friend. Can you think of any reasons for the similarities or the differences that you find ?

EXERCISE IV

1. (This is part of an experiment on the way in which learning is done. It will be continued in later exercises. Notice what happens when you do it.)

Look at these two rows of numbers, and try to learn as many of them as you can in thirty seconds.

2 5 1 0 1 3 1 8 2 1 2 6
2 9 3 4 3 7 4 2 4 5 5 0.

Now write them from memory.

2. Have you ever worked under a person who was " bossy " ? What effect had the bossiness on you or on other members of the group ?

3. You know what is meant by chronological age. You have read in Chapter II something about mental age. It is useful sometimes to know the relationship between the mental age of a pupil and his chronological age. The ratio of one to the other can be expressed conveniently by dividing the mental age by the chronological age. The quotient so obtained is usually multiplied by 100 and called the " intelligence quotient ". If a boy's mental age is 12 and his chronological age is 10, what is his " intelligence quotient " ?

$$\left(\text{The answer is } \frac{12}{10} \times \frac{100}{1} \text{ or } 120.\right)$$

If a boy's mental age is 12 and his chronological age is 12, what is his intelligence quotient ?

4. Here are the marks of six girls in Latin and in Mathematics :

Latin :	25 ;	10 ;	13 ;	18 ;	21 ;	26.
Mathematics :	29 ;	34 ;	37 ;	42 ;	45 ;	50.

What degree of correspondence is there between their success in the two subjects ? Which does best in Latin ?

Which does best in Mathematics ? Which does worst ?

EXERCISE V

1. Have you ever read a story or biography in which a description is given of a teacher and his pupils ? Give some account of the incident you remember best.

Why do you think you remember that incident ?

2. Begin with the word " Home ", and write each word that comes into your mind. Stop writing after two minutes.

Look back at your list and try to think of any possible reason for passing from each word to the next.

3. What, in your opinion, are the characteristics of a good home?

4. What are the chief devices which you have known parents to employ when trying to modify the behaviour of their children?

EXERCISE VI

1. (This is part of the learning experiment you began in exercise IV.

Look at these two rows of numbers, and try to learn as many of them as you can in thirty seconds.

251	013	182	126
293	437	424	550.

Now write them from memory.

2. (Here is the beginning of another experiment on the processes involved in learning. Notice what happens in this also.)

Look at these words and try to learn as many of them as you can in thirty seconds:

mom, te, snem, ntte, nema, tae, mas, aet, meso.

Now write them from memory.

3. If a girl's mental age is 7 and her chronological age is 10, what is her " intelligence quotient "? (A convenient abbreviation for the words " intelligence quotient " is " I.Q.")

4. Write the number 2. Add 3. Write 5. Add 3 to 5. Write the answer. Then add 3 to the answer and keep on adding 3 in that way and writing the answer as fast as you can for two minutes. How far did you get?

5. Look back at the marks given in exercise IV, no 4. Which girl does second best in Mathematics? Which in Latin? What degree of relationship (or " correlation ") do you think there is between success in the two subjects? You can see that it is difficult to express this relationship in words even for so small a number as six pupils.

EXERCISE VII

TO BE CARRIED OUT, IF POSSIBLE, BY A GROUP OF FRIENDS

1. Have you recently tried to learn anything new? Describe, as fully as you can, your reasons for wishing to learn and your experiences while learning.

2. What is your attitude towards the cinema? Write down your own opinion about this.

Now talk to your friends about it and collect opinions from as many people as possible. Look for comparable statements in books and newspapers. Make as long a list as you can of opinions about the cinema.

3. Begin at 2; add 3; then add 3 to your answer and keep on adding 3 for two minutes. How far did you get this time? What happened as you worked?

4. These were the numbers reached by a group of friends who tried what you have just been asked to do:

275, 239, 161, 290, 305, 143, 227, 200, 188.

Arrange these numbers in order. Which is the middle one? (Such a middle number in a series is sometimes called the "median" number.)

EXERCISE VIII

More experiments on learning

1. Look at these words and try to learn as many of them as you can in thirty seconds:

mate, eat, men, tome, Sam, net, so, mess, ten.

Now write them from memory.

2. Look at these numbers and try to discover how they are arranged:

2 5 10 13 18 21 26.

Did you notice that $2 + 3 = 5$, $5 + 5 = 10$, $10 + 3 = 13$, $13 + 5 = 18$ and so on?

Now spend thirty seconds in trying to memorise the numbers below;

2 5 10 13 18 21 26
26 29 34 37 42 45 50.

Write them from memory.

3. Look back at the record of the numbers reached in the adding competition in exercise VII, no. 4. Do you notice the range of the differences between individuals? Such "individual differences" can be noted in the results of most tests.

EXERCISE IX

To be carried out, if possible, by a group of friends

1. Look at these words and try to learn as many of them as you can in thirty seconds:

Tom met ten sane men. Sam ate some meat.

Now write them from memory.

2. Next write what you remember of the words you learned in exercise VI and exercise VIII.

Look back to see what you have forgotten.

3. What differences can you discover between the lists in exercises VI, VIII and IX?

What similarities are there?

Have the differences in the structure of the lists had any effect upon ease of memorising?

4. Do the same with the lists of numbers in exercises IV, VI and VIII.

5. Make a list of the chief activities and occupations which have interested you

(*a*) as a child,
(*b*) during your teens,
(*c*) in adult life.

Did you live in a town or in the country? Compare your list with those of others and consider any differences.

EXERCISE X

1. Look back at the lists of words in exercises VI, VIII, IX.

Which list did you learn most easily? What do you believe to be the reason for its being most easily memorised?

2. Look at the list you have collected of opinions about the cinema. Some of them may be very favourable in their attitude towards it. Some may be very unfavourable, and some may express indifference or neutrality. Write each opinion on a separate slip of paper, and arrange these slips in piles according to the sort of attitude they seem to express. Put all the very favourable ones in one pile. Next to this put all the favourable ones. Then make a pile of the neutral ones, of the unfavourable ones and of the very unfavourable ones. This sorting into five groups is a first step towards the construction of a simple test of attitude towards the cinema.

3. Think of your three best friends. Write down what you believe to be the reasons for your being friendly with each.

4. What do you believe to have been your most terrifying experience? Make a list of any fears you have experienced. Which do you now seem to have outgrown?

EXERCISE XI

1. What personal characteristics in a pupil do you consider most likely to lead towards success in school?

2. Think of the teacher who was most successful in helping you to learn.

What personal characteristics of that teacher contributed most to that success?

3. You have tried rating attitudes on a five-point scale (arranging them into five groups). The same kind of rating can be used in the assessment of personal qualities.

Very strong.	Strong.	Of Medium Strength.	Weak.	Very weak.

Make a five-point rating scale for three of the attributes you mentioned in your answer to question 1 above.

4. If a boy's mental age is $6\frac{1}{2}$ and his chronological age is 10, what is his I.Q.?

5. What is your most unpleasant memory of life in school? Why is it so unpleasant?

EXERCISE XII

1. Look back at the lists of numbers in exercises IV, VI and VIII. Which list did you reproduce most accurately? What do you believe to be the reason for this greater accuracy?

2. Think of something which you have had difficulty in learning recently. Can you suggest a way of applying to it what you have noticed about the easy memorising of numbers or words?

3. Look back over a collection of a series of photographs of yourself (or of someone known to you). What can you discover about the stages through which you (or he) passed? Ask relatives and friends for their recollections of remarks made which might indicate attitudes at different stages.

4. Try to make notes on the behaviour of one friend—an adult or a child—for one hour. What did he do? How many times did he laugh, or cry, or cheat, or lie, or co-operate, or show temper?

5. Think of the person whose advice you are most willing to accept. What do you believe to be the reasons for that willingness?

EXERCISE XIII

An Experiment to try with a group of friends

1. Here is a simple rating scale for four attributes.

Very intelligent.	Intelligent.	Of ordinary brightness.	Rather stupid.	Very stupid.
Very good tempered.	Good-tempered.	Of ordinary stability.	Bad-tempered.	Very ill-tempered.
Very submissive.	Submissive.	Quite well-balanced in behaviour.	Aggressive.	Very dominant.
Very diffident.	Diffident.	Normal.	Confident.	Very confident.

Ask each of your friends to use the scale to rate each one of the group on these four attributes.

2. In the same way try out the five-point scales you devised in exercise XI. Do you all agree in your assessment of every member of the group on each attribute?

3. What do you believe to be your chief interests? Collect lists of such interests from any friends who will co-operate. Can you classify them? Do they change with age? Can you account for their origin?

EXERCISE XIV

1. What, in your opinion, are the most serious types of misbehaviour among children? Choose an example of one and indicate what you consider to be its origins and suitable treatment.

2. Choose one person (child or adult) whom you know well, and make a careful study of formative influences and present state—noting points such as the following:

Formative influences: Position in family. Attitude of parents. Age and educational standards of parents. Emotional atmosphere of home. Religious outlook. Customs of home. Past health. Developmental history (age of weaning, walking, talking, etc.).

School History. Attendances. Attitude to teachers. Attitude of teachers.

Characteristics of neighbourhood. Membership of groups.

Present state: Age. Position in school (or occupation). Attainments. Standardised score in a group test of general mental ability.

Present Health. Manner. Carriage. Appearance in general. Interests. Ambitions. Philosophy of life. Religious awareness.

Successes. Failures. Nervous symptoms. Attitude to teachers (or employers), companions, relatives. Routine of eating and sleeping. Exercise. Attitude of others towards him. Attitude towards criticism. Degree of self-insight. Sense of humour.

INDEX